# Redeeming Your Past and Finding Your Promised Land

Dr. Ray L. Self

All Scripture quotations, unless otherwise indicated from the New American Standard Bible(NASB), © Copyright 1960, 1962, 1963, 1968, 1971, 1972, 1973, 1975, 1977, 1995 by the Lockman Foundation. Used by permission.

Scripture quotations marked (KJV) are from The King James Version (KJV).The KJV is public domain in the United States.

Scripture quotations marked (RSV) are from the Revised Standard Version of the Bible, copyright 1946, 1952, 1971 by the division of Christian Education of the National Council of Churches of Christ in the USA. Used by permission.

ISBN 978-1482654387

# CONTENTS

*"Before I formed you in the womb I knew you, and before you were born I consecrated you; I have appointed you a prophet to the nations."*

*Jeremiah 1:5 (NASB)*

## Dedication

*"Every good gift and every perfect gift is from above, and cometh down from the Father of lights, with whom is no variableness, neither shadow of turning."*

*James 1:17*

I dedicate this book to my beautiful wife, Christie. Her support, patience, and amazing unconditional love always encourage me and give me strength. I deeply appreciate her tender heart and loving prayers. She is truly God's perfect gift for me.

# Introduction

Redeeming your past and finding your promised land are subjects that havebeen in my heart for many years. I have studied and meditated on the various problems that have plagued me, as well as others, and have caused obstacles to peace, fulfillment, and success. I discovered there are many issues still hindering lives and purposes that remain buried within most people. To simply ignore them or deny them is not wise and is definitely not the way of the Lord.

Redeeming your past is about finding the truth from your past and resolving the issues that remain as obstacles for your present, as well as your future. I know some of you may ask, "Why go back and dig up the past?"The answer is obvious. Your past is still affecting your present and helping to determine your future. To ignore the issuesand messages of the past is equivalent to ignoring life itself. Your memories contain treasures as well as pain. Your memories contain informationand wisdom. The apostle Paul wrote that renewing your mind would transform you. The renewing of your mind has to do with your past because your mind contains memories of the past. Your future has yet to affect your mind.

As you read this book, you will learn how to identify and overcome obstacles that are still causing difficulty within your present-day life and, therefore, are hindering you from entering into yourown promised land. Satan has worked hard to destroy you and keep you from God's purpose. Redeeming your past is about restoring God's purpose and hope in your life.

I do not want this book to be a negative review of your past, but rather anhonest look at the damage done to youand to reveal positive ways to restore you to the beautiful image God designed for you. In the book of Nehemiah we find the story of the prophet, Nehemiah who was a captive of the king of Babylonia. He asked the king for permission to return to Jerusalem to restore the wall of his beloved hometown. Because of the king's admiration for Nehemiah, he granted his request and gave him special authority to complete his mission. When Nehemiah arrived in Jerusalem, his first order of business was to ride around the broken down wall and examine the damage.According to Nehemiah 2:17, he said to the people there, "You see the bad situation we are in, that Jerusalem is desolate and its gates burned by fire. Come let us rebuild the wall of Jerusalem so that we will no longer be a reproach" (NASB).Nehemiah was then able to assemble teams and families to rebuild the wall. Only after there had been a damage assessment could the wall be rebuilt. It is much the same with us today. In order to rebuild our lives into the image God has planned for us, there must be a damage assessment. By looking at the damage done, we can determine a strategy for restoring our lives and redeeming our past, therefore allowing us to move into our promised landwithout hindrances.

The purpose of this book is to teach you how to look honestly at anything within your personal belief system or emotional psyche that is hindering you from moving into what the Lord has for you.You will learn how to apply healing,with the help of God, to yourself and any loved one adversely affected by thepast.

A basic premise of life is thatyou will not find true satisfaction or peace until you are working toward your God-created purpose. Over your lifetime, there have been dark forces that have come against you to keep you from what God has purposed for you known as schemes.Satan customizes these schemes just for you. These counter-attacksare against the positive plans of God for your life. In this book, we are going to look at painful facts and examine truths that can set you free.

Facing the negative forces in your life has a major purpose: to deal with these forces and gain freedom so you can move into your purpose. As we examine truth, you will discover truth alone will not make you free. It seems it should, but if you do not add other neededelements, which include His grace and time, truth may simply bring knowledge or condemnation. God can heal instantaneously, but most often, He heals through growth-oriented processes requiring a continual diet of truth, time, and His grace.

Multitudes of books have been written on the subject of helping people overcome obstacles. My perspective may be a little different as I guide you in looking through the perspective of the Word of God and the revelation of the Holy Spirit.

Through my years of ministry, the Lord has allowed me to see His truth about many of His people. Ihave discovered God's truth about an individual is usually much differentfrom what that person is living. I believe it when the Bible says that God's plan for us is "exceedingly abundantly above all"we could think or imagine (Ephesians 3:20).

I want to see every one of God's children living up to the potential God created within him or her. Satan has been working your entire life to keep you from this plan. Satan doesnot attack God directly; he attacks God by hindering His plans for His people. Satan is not concerned about you as an individual; he is concerned about you living up to your God-given potential and helping God complete His plans for His creation.

The reasons to examine your past are many, but the most important reason of all is to be able to complete the assignment God created you to do. You have probably heard it said many times that you are not an accident. You were designed for a purpose, a specific destiny. You were created to do God's work. The world is in a perpetual search for satisfaction. It looks for satisfaction in many ways such as appearance, money, or success. As Christians, we should understand true satisfaction comes only from God, knowing who we are, and doing what we were created to do.

One of the exciting things about living up to your potential is it will amaze you. The capabilities God created within you require more than you can do on your own. God wants the glory so He uses ordinary people in extraordinary ways. God gifts Christians with great authority, power, and responsibility. However, Satan has been attacking Christians through circumstances, lies, and emotional pain to keep them from walking and living in that power and authority. He knows if all Christians lived up to their potential, his reign on Earth would quickly end.

Redeeming your past means searching for doorways that have let Satan have access to your life. It means closing them and blocking his influence. Redeeming your past is about honesty. It takes courage to be honest because you must let go of self-protection and self-justification.

Matthew Hagee, author and minister, said that integrity is transparency. I agree. If we have integrity but we cannot be transparent about our past influences, and ourselves then we are not truly being honest. Being transparent is not easy. However, it must be done in the right circumstance with safe people.

Throughout Scripture, God shows us the importance of confession. We are saved through confession. Romans 10:9 says,"if you confess with your mouth Jesus as Lord, and believe in your heart that God raised Him from the dead, you will be saved." We are forgiven through our confessions. "If we confess our sins, He is faithful and righteous to forgive us our sins and to cleanse us from all unrighteousness" (1 John 1:9).We are healed through our confessions. "Therefore, confess your sins to one another, and pray for one another so that you may be healed" (James 5:16). It is safe to say God expects us to be honest and to confess. Confession is important to God and therefore must be important to each of us. For forgiveness and healing to take place, God requires honesty and confession—not excuses.

God is omnipresent. He has been in our past.He is active in our present. He will be in our future. In the following Scripture, it is interesting to note that God reminds us of our past before He tells us that we will forget it. "Fear not; for thou shalt not be ashamed: neither be thou confounded; for thou shalt not be put to shame: for thou shalt forget the shame of thy youth" (Isaiah 54:4).

God wants us to forget our shame. He reminds us that we have shame in our past to tell us that it is possible to forget it. It is not an actual erasing of a memory, but instead, it is a healing of the pain of the shame and its consequences.

In fact, Jesus endured shame on the cross to bring healing to us. The shame of our past was nailed to the cross with Jesus. "Instead of your shame you will have a double portion, and instead of humiliation they will shout for joy over their portion" (Isaiah 61:7 NASB). The principle of God's forgiveness and healing is admitting there was shame in our past, looking at the causes of it, and then applying God's healing power to it. Whenever there is sin or disobedience, there will always be an element of shame in us. God calls us to deal with shame by admitting it, forsaking it, and then applying His healing principlesthrough Christ.Everything God does must come to us through our faith in Jesus Christ.

I carried much shame from my childhood into my adult life. Mybeliefs about myselfcame from years of condemning messages. The unintended messengers were events, friends, and family.

Every painful circumstance contains messages. When we internalize these messages, they become part of your belief system. This belief system begins to govern your identity. In turn, your identity will govern your life. Your everyday walk—both successes and failures—isprimarily determined by what you think of yourself.

I did not believe I mattered or amounted to much, which translated to a life of frustration. I wanted good things for myself, but inside I did not believe I deserved them. I was striving but never quite getting where I wanted to be because the belief of being unworthy wouldsubconsciously sabotage me.

This book is about revealing what may be hiddenin you and allowing the light of the Spirit of Truth to bring healing. While Satan is a concealer, God is a revealer. The Lord will help you remove the barriers in your life – not only for your sake, but also for the sake of others, so that you can minister to them.

You may question that you have a call into ministry. That is not true. All believers are called to minster to one another and work together to build the Kingdom of God in this world. Ministry occurs at home, at work, at church, and in the community. God's purpose is accomplished in your life by many different methods. It is important to fulfill your purpose for your welfare and for the good of those assigned to your life. It is important to God that you start taking steps toward your call.

# Part One

## Redeeming Your Past

### Chapter One

### What Is Stopping You?

"Before I formed you in the womb I knew you, and before you were born I consecrated you; I have appointed you a prophet to the nations" (Jeremiah 1:5).

In the versequoted above, we can see several important life principles. First, God knew you before you were born. This is important because it lets you know your birth is part of His grand plan. This gives you value and self-worth, which is beyond anything the world can offer. Just to know that God planned for you to be born exactly in His timing and exactly for His purposes can be life changing.

Secondly, God said, "I consecrated you." Before you were born, God already set you apart for a specific purpose. When God consecrates something, it is designed specifically and perfectly for a purpose. There is no one else created to doyour purpose the way God designed you to do it because there is only one you.

Thirdly, God clearly states, "I have appointed you a prophet to the nations." Not only does God know you before you were born and create you for a specific purpose, He wants you to know what that purpose is. In the case of Jeremiah, God created him to be a prophet to the nations. Just like Jeremiah, you are known by God and have been created to be _____. How you fill in this blank is critical to your ultimate success and happiness. The reason for your birth comes from your Creator andis within you.

Your purpose has most likely been under attack your entire life. The reason your past must be redeemed is that there has been a grand scheme of Satan to counterfeit and counterattack God's plan. Satan is more concerned about God's planthan he is about you. What he wants to do is stop God's purpose from manifesting through you. Therefore, Satan works your entire life to keep you from that purpose. He believes if he can slow down or stop you from fulfilling your purpose, he can slow down or stop God's work.

It is important to God and His Kingdom that you deal honestly and fearlessly with anything that comes against God's plan foryour life. There is a war happening in the spirit realm and it concerns you. Satan uses demonic influences against you andhas designed many events and painful circumstances in your life to stop you or destroy your purpose.His weapons are many and he wants to keep his schemes a secret. He knows once a scheme is uncovered, you can stop it. God's truth will reveal these weapons and schemes and His truth is the vehicle for setting you free.

Most of Satan's schemes are buried in the subconscious memory but can manifest into the present. Messages, labels, and events of your past can still have an effect on your present-day life. Not dealing with subconscious issues does not make them go way, but simply allows them to come out in unhealthy and destructive ways. If you do not work to healfrom past painful events and their messages, you are enabling the weaponsformed against you to continue to succeed.

So many people are afraid of looking honestly at themselves because of fragile self-esteem issues. When a person is secure, in whom he is and his purpose as a child of God, then looking at the past and admitting faults and issues is not difficult. A problem arises with people who have fragile self-esteems. These people have created various methods to protect their images.When challenged these methods tend to fail.Many people do not want their defense mechanisms exposed.Because they are afraid to be discovered for who they really are, they have built barriers around themselves. They fear that if people knew the truth about them, they may not be accepted. What they do not understand is God is not interested in their defense mechanisms. He already knows who they really are, and He already accepts them and loves them unconditionally.

Satan loves it when people are not honest and real,when they hide behind masks, because he knows God is a God of truth. Satan also loves it when people arefakingit orput up barriers to protect themselves. He knows these barriers keep all of his schemes, methods, and messages hidden and protected within the souls of his victims.

All of the events of our lives are stored within our subconscious memory. Our subconscious memory is like a computer hard drive, which continually stores datathat is onlyaccessible when the right key is pressed. The button that brings our subconscious memories into our present-daymay vary. For example, my car radio is a catalyst.When I am driving on a long trip, I sometimes like to flip through radio stations. Every now and then, I will stop and listen to an oldies but goodies station. When I hear a song from my high school years, it brings up memories of that season of my past. The stimulus of music from the past brings a memory to the present. Those memories can be good or bad and likewise hold good and bad feelings.

I believe Satan uses painful events to create harmful effects. Events like these can create painful memories we want to forget and can lead to unhealthy messages turning into false beliefs. That is why it is important we take this journey of discovery, so these messages will not have long-term effects.

Here is an example: I heard a story, not long ago, about a little girl abused by her uncle. As she walked across the room one day, her uncle commented on the pretty, yellow blouse she was wearing. They were alone and the uncle touched her in an inappropriate way. For the rest of her life, the girl lived with tremendous guilt. The lie she believed was that somehow because she was wearing a pretty blouse, she shared in the guilt of the sexual abuse.

As you can see in this story, when abuse takes place, it is horrible. There is great pain. In addition, because of the messages, labels, and self-judgments that often come with it, there can be long-term suffering. In the story just told, the young girl thought she shared in the responsibility of the abuse and as a result, she was a bad person.That self-judgment hindered herand kept her from all that God had for her. People like this girl, who believe they are bad, have a hard time believing they could be accepted by God.

Events of the past can cause painful wounds. These wounds can create false labels. These labels can lead to false beliefs. In addition,for better or worse, what we believe governs our lives. The girl in the story labeled herself a bad person.For the rest of her life, she believed that label. The implications of that belief were devastating.

It is important we each look at our past anduncover our own false labels and self-judgments. Self-judgment is nearly always in direct contradiction to God's judgment. Remember, God has judged us as righteous because of His Son's amazing sacrifice. "He made Him who knew no sin to be sin on our behalf, so we might become the righteousness of God in Him"(2 Corinthians 5:21).

Self-judgment usually develops because of a message that came from painful events. Internal messages are created in many ways. For example, a child of divorced parents will often think if his parents had loved him enough, they would not have divorced. The message the child may believe is,"I am unlovable." "I am unworthy of love." This message can easily turn into a labeland the label can turn into a belief. When the child grows up, he still believeshe is not worthy of love, which causes great damage in relationships he enters into. Often he is drawn into unhealthy relationships, because he honestly does not feel he deserves healthy and good ones. Unhealthy relationships can even feel normal and comfortable. When he happens to enter into a healthy relationship, typically he will subconsciously sabotage it, because he still believes he is not worthy of love.

Another example of a damaging message leading to wrong beliefs is found among children who are continually disciplined and not nurtured. If a child is continually disciplined, and not nurtured this is a formula for disaster. Without the affirmation of nurturing parents,a child begins to believe he can never measure up. Each mistake he makes and his parents resulting discipline reinforce this belief. In my experience, in every case where I have witnessed strict parents who fail to nurture a child,that child will end up rebelling.

There are numerous damaging messages that can arise when a child is abandoned by his parents. The messages may be, "I am unlovable; I am unworthy; I am not valuable." With an abused child, the messages are much the same.The point is that most pain contains a message. The message can turn into a label and the label can turn into a belief. A label can be defined as a personal identity. Just as all products in a store have labels to tell us what they are; a personal label tells an individual who he is. A label can be true or false. When false labeling occurs, what the person believes about himself is very different from what God believes about him.God wants our unwavering faith to be only in Him and in what He says about us.

Think about this in your own life. Do you know yourself well enough to be able to write down what you honestly believe about yourself? It is amazing how many distorted images we can hold of ourselves. If we do not base our belief systems on the Word of God, then we are at the mercy of our experiences and their messages. The world's system confirms these messages, because the world is normally in opposition to God's Word.

The Bible is very clear about God's view of us. Over 230 Scriptures in the New Testament alone identify how God sees us. For example, we have been born again as children of God; we are joint heirs with Jesus Christ; and we are members of the royal priesthood. The devil does not want us to have this knowledgebecause he knows if we honestly believe what God says about us, itwill change our lives and destroy his power over us.

The process of redeeming your past takes honestyand courage. This will be easier for some than for others. For those of you who feel blocked in taking an honest assessment of yourselves, I ask you to simply pray and ask the Holy Spirit to show you what you need to know. Some of you may even have a fear of doing that. Be assured, God will let you know what you need to know; it will not hurt you; itwill be for your ultimate good.

Honesty, transparency, and confessing our faults can hurt a little bit, but the result is well worth it. Dealing with issues can be painful, but not all pain is harmful. Remember, the goal is to rid the obstacles and move on unhindered into your promised land. It is here that you will find peace and fulfillment.When you know you are who God says you are and you are doing what God created you to do it is a wonderful way of life.

Review Questions –

Why do many people struggle with looking honestlywithin themselves?

Based on your experiences, what weapons have been formed against you?

What do you believe about yourself? Are any of these beliefs possibly distorted? Do these beliefs agree with God's view of you? If not, what does God say?

Do you believe God created you for a specific purpose? Do you know what that purpose is? If so, describe it.

# Chapter Two

## Truth, Grace and Time

In Dr. Henry Cloud's book, *Changes that Heal*, he mentions what he refers to as three elements for growth. These three things are very important because if one is missing, there is a growth problem. In your discovery process, as you get honest with yourself with the help of the Lord, you will definitely discover issues that need dealt with and healed so you can enter into your personal promised land.

Upon discovering an issue, you must face the truth. You will also have choices to make concerning your well-being. You will discover things that can be painful or even a little scary, yet they are the truth about your past and explain some of the effects in your present-day life. Truth in itself would seem to be all we need. Jesus said, "...and you will know the truth, and the truth will make you free" (John 8:32). Jesus also made it clear He is the truth. "Jesus said to him, 'I am the way, and the truth, and the life; no one comes to the Father but through Me'" (John 14:6).

The principle from these scriptures indicates clearly that truth can make us free. The truth Scripture is referring to is Jesus Christ Himself who is the truth. This truth refers to who He is and what He taught us and includes His power working in us through the Holy Spirit. Yes, indeed truth can make you free. Jesus spoke truth continually, teaching us God's requirements in the new covenant. He taught us what salvation really is. Most of all, He died for us to give us the grace and forgiveness we need in order for God's truth to work in us.

You see, Jesus spoke truth and taught the truth. He knew the world needed to hear truth that would set them free, but Jesus also knew something else. The world needed more than just truth. The world needed grace, so Jesus went to the cross and offered His own body as a perfect sacrifice in the ultimate act of grace. Yes, Jesus said the truth would set you free, but Jesus knew the truth alone would not work without the grace of God. It is the same in our lives. To be healed and freed from all the issues that hold us back we need the truth, but it will take the grace of God for true healing to take place.

The grace of God tells us we are okay, even now. The grace of God allows us to be loved unconditionally regardless of where we are in our growing and healing process. The grace of God allows us to have access to God Himself, to come into His presence and seek His very hand for our help. The grace of God is the greatest gift ever given to mankind, but it only applies to those who believe in and accept Jesus Christ as their Savior. Jesus was the truth and He spoke truth, but He loved us so much that He gave us the ultimate gift of God's grace.

The grace of God allows us to be okay now. The grace of God allows us to be acceptable now. The grace of God gives us our self-esteem and assurance we can make it and we donot have to wait for the future to be loved and acceptable. God loves us just as we are, no strings attached. Becauseof His love, He will not leave us as we are.

Without grace, it is so easy to fall into condemnation. On the voyage of discovery, you are likely to find faults, past sins, personal failures, and events that caused you to be the victim or even the perpetrator. The discovery and realization can be shocking. At first, they can even seem discouraging. If a person does not know and understand God's unconditional love and have their value rooted in what God's Word says, they can easily fall into condemnation and the trap of guilt and shame. God's pours out His grace upon all believers the moment they accept Jesus Christ and His finished work. The believer's faith is in the fact that Jesus Christ went to the cross and died for the sins of all humankindand that will set them free and allow God's grace to pour out.

Jesus took so much to the cross it is hard to comprehend. The Bible says He knew no sin, but then He became sin and gave us His righteousness. "He made Him who knew no sin to be sin on our behalf, so we might become the righteousness of God in Him" (2 Corinthians 5:21). He took what belonged to us and then gave us what rightfully belonged to Him. He took our sin and in exchange gave us His righteousness. This righteousness puts us in right standing with God and gives us access to Him. This act of grace powerfully demonstrates God's unconditional love for us.

How much does God love you? Well, how much valuable was the life of Jesus Christ? This was the price paid for you! All believers are worth the price of the life of Jesus Christ. Knowing who you are and knowing whom you belong to, creates a confidence, not in yourself alone, but a confidence in the new creation God made in you when you are born again.

God's grace gives us the love and acceptance we need while we are in the healing process. Healing can be painful, so we will all need doses of God's love as we go through the process of redeeming our past.

"For if by the transgression of the one, death reined through the one, much more those who receive the abundance of grace and of the gift of righteousness will rein in life through the One, Jesus Christ" (Romans 5:17). This gift of the abundance of grace and God's righteousness allows us to conquer anything life has ever thrown at us. We have available to us the grace and love of God to get us through anything that has caused us to fall short of God's plans and purposes.

Just because you have fallen short and maybe have not accomplished everything God created you to do, it does not mean you are unacceptable or unlovable. Remember, God's love is unconditional and this love is not waiting for you to get it together; it is available for you right now. From this position of strength, you can move freely and confidently into any area needing healing.

The third thing needed is time. You can know the truth about what the issue is, where the pain originated and you can have God's unconditional love to help you get through all of this, but this will also take time. I love when things conclude instantaneously, but I know that is not always, what is best for me. God's world and His created living beings are in a continual growth process. None of us like to go through processes; we all love instant gratification, but that normally does not help us mature. In the growth process, roots are established and strength gained. In the growth process, we learn about the Lord and ourselves. When we allow God to take His time and work in His perfect season, the results are wonderful.

Healing takes time, truth, and God's grace. If one of these elements is missing, then problems will arise. If it is all grace and there is no truth, then we will allow ourselves to go in any direction with no consequence. This can have disastrous results. If it is all truth and no grace, we will surely fall into condemnation and shame. In addition, if we do not give everything the time it needs, no real growth can take place.

Often we believe confessing the sin and asking God to heal will cause instantaneous change. In actuality, quick change sometimes results, but normally God wants us to learn, grow, and become stronger and wiser over time.

In actuality, we are rightfully healed and delivered from disease, sin, shame, condemnation, poverty, and all curses. These and many more are victories Christ won at the cross. The task for all Christians is that through faith and abiding in God, we allow these victories to begin to manifest in our lives.

According to the Book of Proverbs, as a man thinks in his heart so is he. When our faith becomes our reality, our lives aredramatically changed. Everything in life centers on our faith in Jesus Christ. Ultimately, all healing and answers to every problem is found in Him.

"For by grace you have been saved through faith; and that not of yourselves, it is the gift of God" (Ephesians 2:8). A very important key point to understand is we are saved by grace not by works, which is actually contrary to human nature. The concept of grace that God talks about in His Word is really a foreign concept to our nature. We are raised to believe everything has a cost in this world and the price must be paid if we are to have anything of value. This principle is implanted in us at an early age. As youngsters, to earn money, we would have to do our chores in order that we gain our allowance. As teenagers, we probably took our first part-time job so we could have money in order to have some fun. As adults, we work to earn a living to pay for home, our credit cards, our car, and our everyday expenses. It seems everything we get in life comes through our work. This programming runs deep within us. So now we have the greatest thing we could ever have, our salvation, and it comes as a gift of grace. Our human nature says we must earn this in some way. Many people mistakenly believe they can earn God's grace and His salvation by being good. If they do right and treat people well, then they will go to heaven. The problem with this is that the ticket to heaven now has a price, which is not very much. Even though God is offering us something by grace, our nature is still trying to earn it. I believe this is actually an insult to God. What God is offering to us is so incredibly valuable that not all of the money or wealth in the world could purchase it. Our attempt to purchase salvation by our own personal goodness devalues the salvation of Jesus Christ to a very low level. Salvation must be by God's grace, not by works; therefore, noone gets credit, except for God.

This unearned amazing grace is exactly what we need to for our healing. Salvation has a benefit package and one of the key benefits is grace for our own personal healing. God's plan is for us to be healed and set free so we can move quickly, powerfully, and successfully into the purpose He has for us. God's plan for us will happen through showing us the truth, giving us His unlimited grace, and allowing us the time necessary for all these things to take place.

I encourage you not to shortcut the process. Find the truth about what is hindering you. Receive God's grace and love that will keep you secure while being healed. Then give yourself plenty of time. God uses a necessary process to heal all of us.

Jesus spoke the truth but demonstrated the ultimate act of grace. He has given us over 2000 years to grow, to learn, and become all He wants us to be. Your healing and freedom istied to Christ because everything in life ultimately is about Him. It is time to redeem your past and find your promised land!

Review questions –

Truth can set us free, but why must truth be combined with grace?

Are you able to give yourself the same grace God gives you? Explain.

What is the relationship between time and healing?

How does a Christian obtain what the Scripture promises?

# Chapter Three

## Hunger

Hunger, according to Daniel Webster, is to feel the pain or uneasiness, which is occasioned by a long abstinence from food; to desire with great eagerness; to crave.

No one likes to be hungry. Hunger happens when you are away from something you desire for too long. We were born with hunger. Hunger for food, hunger for love, hunger for acceptance, hunger for money, hunger for contentment. The list could be very long. Hunger drives humanity. Hunger for money, hunger for fame, hunger for power, hunger for significance, and hunger for satisfaction.

An interesting thing about the hunger the world is so involved in is it is never satisfied. You never hear of someone saying, "I have enough money," or "I have enough success." Ultimately, everyone wants more and more. When hunger is not satisfied, the craving continues. The hunger the world system perpetuates is a hunger not satisfied so, therefore, it continues in a never-ending search for fulfillment.

There are thousands and perhaps millions of examples of this, i.e., athletes who refuse to retire because they found their fulfillment in sports achievement or multi-millionaires who continue to make a profit even though they have more money than they could ever use. There are young people who drift in and out of relationships with the hunger for affection thinking the romantic love of another person will bring them complete satisfaction. In world history, there are countless stories of dictators and kings who were not satisfied with their own land and, therefore, their hunger motivated them to conquer other countries.

Misdirected hunger is like walking on a treadmill: a lot of exhorted effort, but you never get anywhere. Hunger is an incredible motivator. People will go to great lengths and extremes to satisfy their hunger. No matter what the hunger is for it simply has to exist in order to drive humanity. I believe our hunger has been twisted and perverted, which has caused us to look for types of satisfaction and contentment that we can never achieve on our own.

It all started in the Garden of Eden. Adam did not want to be an image of God, he wanted be God. Satan lied to Adam and Eve and because of their misdirected hunger, they rebelled against their Creator. "For God knows that in the day you eat from it your eyes will be opened, and you will be like God, knowing good and evil" (Genesis 3:5). This started a downward spiral of humanity attempting to achieve only what God can provide.

True contentment, satisfaction, and peace come through a relationship with God. However, in his fallen nature, man continually looks in other directions for his satisfaction. It is a huge demonic trap. This hunger is never fulfilled, which causes people to waste their time, energy, and resources trying to satisfy it. The results are disastrous. People, families, communities, and even entire nations are hurt. Countries are devoured by other countries. The rich have more than enough while the poor are starving. Valuable priorities are lost. Misdirected hunger ignores what is most important.

Hunger not put under the control of the Holy Spirit will be driven by our human nature and will cause us to fall into a trap. I call this the "trap of never enough." Never enough money, never enough clothes, never enough things, never enough love, never enough success, never enough happiness, never enough of anything. This "trap of never enough" can ruin lives. The trap keeps people away from what God has for them. It keeps people from finding thepeace, satisfaction, andsuccessthat God wants them to have. This futile search for satisfaction goes on and on, driving man deeper into the depth of materialism. Material things can be nice, they can be temporarily fun, but no "thing" will ever make you happy. Things do not bring life, peace, and satisfaction. The desire for things creates an illusion that if a person possesses these particular things, then they will be happy. Yet, when the possession is achieved, the hunger is still there.

"Delight yourself in the LORD; And He will give you the desires of your heart" (Psalm 37:4). This is the answer to twisted hunger. In order to have the right desire, the promise of God says if we delight ourselves in the Lord and if we make the Lord our priority, then He will plant His desires within us. When your personal hunger comes into agreement with the Lord's desires, great things will result in your life. Hunger is a powerful motivating force when directed toward God amazing things can be accomplished. God will begin to give you new vision with new desires that will powerfully motivate your life.

I believe man's natural hunger is carnal in nature. I am not talking about a lack of food. I am referring to our desires. The trap of this desire is the thinking that if I get what I want, then I will be happy. When I was young, I would go from one desire to another. I remember as a teenager wanting a guitar more than anything.I pictured me playing the guitar like the Beatles or Jimi Hendrix. I pictured myself as a true rock 'n roll musician. I knew, or thought I knew, that would make me happy and not to mention very cool. My mother purchased a guitar and lessons for me. I had difficulty though. The first problem was I did not have much of an ear for music. The second problem was I had no rhythm. My dream was,pretty much, unattainable. My balloon eventually burst. I thought the guitar would make me happy and make me very cool. I got what I wanted only to find out it was an illusion.

As I grew into adulthood, I had many dreams and desires I thought would bring me satisfaction and contentment. In my college days, I thought I could find contentment with girls. I also thought I could find contentment with being the coolest person on campus.

Repeatedly I tried, but I was never content. Later, I thought money would do it, so I went to work. I thought more money would do it, so I sought after promotions. I thought having an important job title would bring me fulfillment. Unbelievably, I became a men's fashion buyer for large department stores. I thought that would do it, but I wasnot satisfied. My hunger continued. I then opened my own clothing store thinking that being a successful entrepreneur would satisfy my hunger. When that fell apart, I took a job as a bookkeeper at an appliance store. It was not what I wanted, but I was desperate. My hunger continued until promoted to the position of a commissioned salesperson. I began making good money. I remember as a young man in the 1970's selling appliances and having $6000 in my checking account. Boy, I thought I was something. However, I was still hungry.

I took a job with the Frigidaire Appliance Company as a district manager. Now, I was in the big leagues! I had a company car, which they replaced every year with a new one. I had an expense account and a company credit card. I attended sales meetings in the Bahamas and Las Vegas. I was successful. I had money. I had a position, but I was still hungry.

I decided to start my own retail store. I went in partnership with a business associate. The little store did over a million dollars in sales the first year. However, I was still hungry. The store fell apart – partly because of my faults and not managing money correctly and partly because of my partner who pulled out and sold his slice of the partnership. I continued to search. I was still hungry. The story could continue. I started another business, which provided custom computer programming services. I worked with some amazing clients, such as Holiday Inn, but still I was not satisfied. I even sat in the offices of Graceland to propose a computer inventory control system to manage all of Elvis's stuff.My hunger was still not satisfied.

To shorten the story, God allowed my life to fall apart. Finally, I reached out to Him as never before and He answered me. I will tell you more about this later in the book. In short, I went back to college, but it was a Bible college. I started getting invitations to teach and to preach the Word of God, which led to my hunger going away. I had spent years hungering for things that I thought would bring me satisfaction, but the hunger was not satisfied. I continued to search and search and search and finally, when I found God and His purpose for my life, I found contentment.

There are key questions I had to confront and you must answer as well:What are you hungering for? Do you desire something that can actually never be completely satisfied? Are your desires ones that will never bring you contentment? If what you are looking for is about what the world system can offer you, you will always be hungry. When you go God's direction with God's purpose, you find the peace and satisfaction you desperately need. If you remain discontented, you will continually search and the devil will help you look in all the wrong directions. Again, the question is, what are you hungry for? Is what you desire coming from God or coming from your carnality? If your hunger and desires are not God's desires, fulfillment is not there. Let me say that again – fulfillment is not there.

I want to close with this thought. The issue of Godly desire is very important, especially when it comes to our youth. I challenge you to stop asking young people what it is they want to do. I cringe every time I hear adults speak to a college student and ask him or her that question. Throughout my life, I wanted to do all sorts of things. Eventually, I learned that when my desires equal God's desires, it is only then that will I be content and fulfilled. This is true of young people today. It is not a question of what they want to do; it is a question of what has God created them to do. This question needs an answer in order for our young people, and all of us, to lead successful, fulfilled, and contented lives.

Long periods of misdirected desire cause Godly desire to be hidden. If you cannot get in touch with God's desire for your life, do not be discouraged. The desire is present but probably buried deep within the soul. This can make the problem of discovery more difficult. God's desire for you will always be there, even if it is dormant. Be assured God wants to bring what is dead back to life. The power of the Holy Spirit can dig up and resurrect desires, long-ago buried deep within your soul. God loves to resurrect anything that is of Him.

God knows our desires are great motivators. If we surrender to the Lord and ask Him, He will put His desires within our hearts. Wanting what God wants fills all the emptiness within our souls. God wants to help us. He knows our struggles. God simply wants us to ask Him, believe in Him, and trust Him. God can change what you desire and bring you satisfaction. Redeeming your past and finding your promised land is going to involve a check- up of your heart and its desires. The issue is what are you hungering for? Only you can answer that question.

Review questions –

Why is hunger such a powerful motivator?

What is the difference between Godly desire and fleshy desire?

How does Satan work to misdirect hunger?

What personal hunger in your life may not be from God? What will you do about it?

# Chapter Four

## Shaping Your Life

Some people say we are a result of all of our experiences. I would say that is probably true for most of us. Everyone has a history and everyone has a story. I used to think my story was tough and more painful than most anybody else's until I began to listen intently to other people. Through years of counseling in ministry, working in personal and group settings, I have heard many tales. I thought my story was bad until I would go to a group session and hear other people's testimonies. It is astounding what people have experienced and gone through. With some people, I am amazed they are still in existence. Considering what they have been through,I am amazed many people are still standing, breathing, and talking. Everyone has had painful disappointments, but also many victories.

Life experiences tend to shape us. I believe the formula that carves out our personhood works something like this: There was a life experience. Perhaps it was traumatic. The experience carried a message with it. The message is believed whether the message is positive or negative. This belief becomes part of a person's identity. That personal identity determines much of the success or failure of that person's life.

Messages can be unheard, but still internalized. I have listed below some typical events and corresponding messages. Some of these concern my own past. For example, when I was a very young baseball player, my mother was sometimes over an hour late inpicking me at the baseball field. The unspoken message was that I was unworthy and not important.

When there is constant criticism, involving being told what is wrong but not being commended or affirmed, the message can be, "You do not measure up. You are not good enough"

You were hurt in a relationship—Message—you are rejected or unlovable.

You were abandoned by a parent—Message—you are unacceptable or unimportant.

You lost a job—Message—you are unqualified, you are unworthy.

You were abused—Message—you deserved it. God does not love

me. You are guilty or shameful.

You were hurt by a church—Message—you are rejected by God and Christians cannot be trusted.

You had a failure—Message—you are a failure.

You made a mistake—Message—you are a mistake.

You were wrong about something—Message—you are a wrong person.

Everyone's past contains messages. Some of these messages contain pain, which can lead to anger, depression, addictions, false personalities, and defense mechanisms. The sin of omission causes a message that is subtle but powerful. It is not what happened to you, but it is what failed to happen. Missing the essentials needed for our devolvement can carry a message. Everyone needs affirmation, love, acceptance, encouragement, and guidance. When omitted these elements, what is left carries a strong message. These messages can be rejection, unworthiness, or the feeling of being unlovable. All of this leads to low self-esteem issues. These messages get into our soul. It is not a logical thought process, but something felt internally and therefore believed; it becomes a part of who we are.

Our creator designed us for love, value and affirmation. God put these needs within us. He intended for our parents to be a representation of His true image. Some parents do this very well, but sadly, many parents have weaknesses in this area. Without having our basic needs met, any person will naturally try to fill those voids. The problem becomes two-fold: the absence of a need and the vain attempts to replace what only God can give. These vain attempts tend to complicate the problem.

Our failure to get what we desperately need creates another set of messages. I am missing something, something is not right, and therefore, I must not be right. I failed; therefore, I must be a failure. I was wrong; therefore, I am a wrong person. These messages are like carving tools that create an image of us formed by experiences. The image literally seems to be set in stone. However, remember, God can remove stones!

Take a moment and take a picture of your image. What do you look like? What is your character? Describe yourself. Then ask the question – does this image of you reflect the image that Scripture describes of a child of God? Are you in disagreement with God concerning who you are? It is important to be able to accept yourself wherever you are in your journey.

Yes, our image is going to fall short of God's view, but that is not a place for condemnation. It is a time for love and acceptance. Accepting who we are now, not who we think we should be. All of us are a portrait painted by God, but not finished. Unconditional love and acceptance comes from God and should come from ourselves.It is important to be able to accept yourself where you are today. All of us will continue to grow and heal, but we must love ourselves now in this moment. By accepting ourselves today, we prepare ourselves for tomorrow.

Most people are in disagreement with God's view of themselves because of a life formed and shaped by various messages. I believe the messages were part of a grand scheme by Satan to destroy your identity and defeat your purpose. It was never you the devil was after, it was your purpose. Christians fulfilling their call from God is the greatest threat to the kingdom of darkness.

Somehow, the devil really seems to target Christians who have a strong anointing. You are a target with specially designed weapons aimed at you. The special weapons are very effective in reinforcing the lies from the messages of your personal life.

Loving yourself where you are means you accept your present state no matter how mistaken it may be, while at the same time knowing God has a plan for your healing, growth, and development. God loves and accepts you where you are, but He will not leave you as you are.

Review questions –

How has your past shaped you?


Are there any messages that you have believed concerning yourself that are not true?


What weapons have been formed against you?



What does it mean to unconditionally love yourself?

# Chapter Five

## Schemes

A scheme may be defined a purposeful plan. Satan, who is the father of lies and a murderer, has designed a plan specifically for you. Designed for you when he finds an effective weapon, herepeatedly continues touse it. Before I continue, I want to acknowledge my pastor, Joe Warner, and his powerful teaching on this subject, which has influenced this chapter.

"Every weapon formed against you shall not prosper" (Isaiah 54:17b). This scripture plainly points out that weapons will be custom designed to come against you. Ultimately, they will not succeed because of the victory that Christ has already won. The Bible also points out that we should be aware of the plans of Satan. Second Corinthians 2:11 says, "In order that Satan might not outwit us. For we are not unaware of his schemes."

Each scheme or plot has its own characteristics designed for a particular person. A scheme is a custom plan that remains hidden, but which is overtly destructive and continually reinforced throughout a person's life. Satan and his demonic horde have plans for your destruction. Once you become aware of these schemes, you will see patterns throughout your history give evidence of them. Some may say this is just a fable, but not according to Scripture and not according to the evidence in people lives.

These schemes can operate from generation to generation. They will grow stronger and continually built upon. There can be a primary scheme as well as a secondary scheme. In the demonic realm, there will always be one particular strongman. It is much like the army with its command structure. The good news is when you take down a leader, you can destroy the enemy's power.

The "root" of most schemes is found early on in a person's life. Schemes usually begin early and can last a lifetime if they are not defeated. Schemes based upon lies afeed upon internal belief systems. The Bible says faith comes by hearing. Unfortunately, lies become believablewhen heard often enough.

The scheme of illegitimacy is the most common scheme. This plan is to invalidate you. All people need a sense of value. We need affirmation, to feel valued, respected, and treasured. Satan seeks to invalidate us at a deep level. By not knowing and respecting our God-given identity, a person will naturally seek validation through other means. Our only true value, which is the greatest value, comes from our Creator, God who values His children so much He even paid for their lives with the life of His son Jesus.

People trying to find value through the world's system is evidence of the fruit of this game of illegitimacy in our society.It is a very sad story because what the world values changes on a daily basis. When you step back and take an objective look at it, you can see clearly the world used actors, people we call stars or celebrities. The world values people with money, power, and fame. The world values athletes when they win the game and devalues athletes who lose. The world values beauty and devalues people who are not. The world values people who have success in society and devalues those who are not successful. The world values people who are cool or part of the in-crowd and devalues people who are not cool. The world values thin people, but not overweight people. The world even values certain races and skin colors above others. You can see from the above-mentioned world systems that this is truly a sickness.

When a person attempts to gain self-esteem and value through an illegitimate way, such as money or appearance, this is actually evidence of the spirit of illegitimacy. God made us legitimate by giving His own Son on thecross to die for us and then He adopted us as His own children. We are, as Christians, children of the King of kings and Lord of lords. Our value cannot be greater than this. Our Creator loves and accepts unconditionally.When we try to gain value through other worldly methods, we are simply feeding the spirit of illegitimacy.

It is very sad people fall into this trap because it is a game never won, a task never completed, so therefore, people spend their lives trying to obtain the unobtainable and waste their days here on Earth. Everyone needs to feel valid, but the only validation that will ever remain is a validation given to us by our Divine Creator.

This scheme can have serious consequences. In order to accomplish our purpose and find the fulfillment that only God can provide, we must know who we truly are and learn to love and embrace only that identity. When a person feels illegitimate, the search for validation is endless. The devil will continually send messages to reinforce his scheme.

The illegitimate spirit will cause us to look for illegitimate ways to find validation. Since the only true validation can come from the One who made us, this search will be fruitless and will waste much valuable time. The spirit of illegitimacy has motivated people and even nations from the beginning of history. Men try to prove their manhood. Nations try to prove their strength and identity.

Another scheme is rejection, which seems to be a common scheme. A person with this scheme seems to be like rejection looking for a place to happen. It appears, wherever this person goes, rejection follows. If there is no rejection, they will attract it.

My scheme is called the "I don't matter scheme." It started at a very young age when my father was a traveling salesman and was gone from Monday through Friday. My mother was ill and could not completely take care of my two sisters and me. My father was a member of the generation called the Greatest Generation. He grew up during the depression and fought in World War II. He experienced four years of combat during the war.He really was an American hero. He was a true "tough guy" and a man's man. My dad believed the correct way to raise a child was to tell them what they were doing wrongand he wasvery good at this. He would correct me any time I failed in his eyes. He could be very strict, had a terrible temper, and would get angry especially when I dropped a baseball or fumbled a football. Now do not get me wrong, he was a great father and very unselfish; he provided every financial need of our family. He was a hard-working man, but the elements I missed were validation and nurturing. My mother was too sick to validate and nurture me, and my father only knew to correct me. He never told me what I did right and he never told me he was proud of me. He never told me he knew I could accomplish much. These words just never came out of his mouth. It was strange because I would hear him brag on some of the neighborhood boys, but not on me. I was told he did brag on me later in life but I never heard it – it was always to other people. It was interesting he did not brag on me to my face.

Every young man needs the validation and approval of the earthly father. I did not have that so it caused me to feel unimportant. I craved approval. I craved acceptance. I did not have either one of those instilled in me as a young man. In high school, I felt inferior. I believed others were much more worthy than I was. I did not believe my thoughts or opinions really mattered. I think you can see where this is going. At age 18,I went into drugs. I did not know why I liked the drugs. I was not aware of something called schemes, but I knew that I felt better when I was high than I did when I was sober.

Because I did not feel important or that I mattered, I worked hard to prove myself, but in very destructive ways. I tried to become the ultimate cool rocker. Later as I married and had children, I tried to find my validation in the business world and with material goods, but theproblem always lingered. I never felt validated or satisfied, so I kept striving to find success and I became more and more frustrated. The change in my life came when I had an encounter with the Holy Spirit in 1986 in what I call the baptism of the Holy Spirit. The power of God came upon me one evening and changed my life in a dramatic fashion from there on.

However, the evidence of the scheme in my life was still seen in everyday events. Whenever I was in a circumstance, where I felt ignored, pain and anger would always rise up against me. I remember being in a men's clothing department of a local department store and needing help to find a particular size and noticing that the salespeople were gathered behind a counter chatting with each other and ignoring me. I was so angry and frustratedI was ready to throw something at them. When I was in a restaurant and the server would not come to the table when I needed her, I would become angry. Any situation where I felt ignoredwould trigger something in me. If I was speaking to someone and that person interrupted me, I felt ignored and would feel the anger rise up within me. All of this is evidence of the scheme, which wasa plot to destroy me and keep me from God's purpose. Because I have become aware of this scheme, I donot fight in the fleshinstead,I fight the real culprit who is the devil. I have a definite purpose and I know what it is. Looking back on my life, it is clear to me that all this work of Satan was to keep me from the place I am in now. I have won a victory and the purpose of this book is to share it with you.

*"For though we walk in the flesh, we do not war according to the flesh, for the weapons of our warfare are not of the flesh, but divinely powerful for the destruction of fortresses. We are destroying speculations and every lofty thing raised up against the knowledge of God, and we are taking every thought captive to the obedience of Christ" (2 Corinthians10:3-5).*

A scheme is always repeated, especially if it is effective. The good news is that there is an easy way to discover a scheme. Do you have destructive patterns in your life? Is there something that seems to be constantly hounding you? Maybe it is the fear of abandonment or maybe it is feeling constantly unworthy or unlovable. Maybe your scheme is simply fear and you have struggled with this problem as long as you can remember.

A good question to ask yourself would be, "Is there a particular message that comes to you through various circumstances and even through well-meaning family and friends?" Does this message tend to repeat itself like an old broken record? Does it just seem like whatever you do and wherever you go you are hit with the same feeling repeatedly? When a wound is constantly reopened, it does not heal.

The devil will take advantage of the various methods of the dysfunctional family to create a scheme. Perhaps there was no nurturing in your family or maybe there were parents who abandoned you. So, it seems throughout your life, wherever you go, you are consistently in relationships with people who tend to abandon you and cannot show you unconditional love. All of these are part of the grand scheme by Satan to keep you away from the plan that God has for you. When you step back and take an objective look at the scheme against your life, you can see how it has been a continual hindrance all of your days.

Knowledge is a vital key to defeating a scheme. Once you are aware of Satan's strategy against you, you can take a firm stand through the Word of God in prayer and resist the schemes. The Word of God clearly says in James 4:7, "Submit therefore to God. Resist the devil and he will flee from you." The first thing we must do as Christians is to submit and surrender ourselves to the Lord. It is in this state of humility and faith that the hand of God moves on our behalf. Without dependence upon the Lord, we are depending solely upon our own strength and, in a sense, actually binding the hand of God. The Lord is not an enabler and if we want to do things in our own strength, He will let us, until we become so tired and burned out that we realize we must rely on Him. Steponeis to fully realize we can do nothing that matters without God's help.

The next thing to do is to expose the lies. Ephesians 5:11 says, "And do not participate in the unfruitful deeds of darkness, but instead even expose them." To expose a lie you must first discuss it. This means you will bring it to the light by describing it. By describing it, you will be able to see clearly, what the lie is and become able to replace it with accurate truth. It is hard to defeat something when you have no clear definition of what it is. If you struggle in this area, simply asked the Holy Spirit to reveal to you the schemes and He will do that for you. The Holy Spirit is the spirit of truth and He loves to expose the lies of the devil and reveal to you the truth of God that replaces that lie. The primary weapon to defeat a scheme is the Word of God. It is what Jesus used in His desert wandering. If this weapon and tactic is good enough for the Lord Jesus, it is surely good enough for us. There is truth in the Word of God that can contradict any lie or scheme against your life.

There are many resources available about the promises of God. Some of these resources give you promises for every circumstance. My advice to you is to find Scripture that reaffirms you, validates you, and defeats the lies coming from the schemes. This part of the war you must fight. It isalsogood to have counselingand to have others praying for you, but ultimately, you must stand for your own rights as a Christian. Here is a listing of typical schemes and answers –

Abandonment:The lie– "People always leave me; noone will be there for me."

> The truth– "Make sure your character is free from the love of money and being content with what you have, for He Himself has said, 'I WILL NEVER DESERT YOU, NOR WILL I EVER FORSAKE YOU'" (Hebrews 13:5).

Illegitimacy:  The lie –"I am not valid. I am not affirmed or valuable in any way".

> The truth– "But you are A CHOSEN RACE, A royal PRIESTHOOD, A HOLY NATION, A PEOPLE FOR God's OWN POSSESSION, so that you may proclaim the excellencies of Him who has called you out of darkness into His marvelous light" (1Peter 2:9).

Rejection:  The lie – "I am always rejected".

> The truth– "No man will be able to stand before you all the days of your life. Just as I have been with Moses, I will be with you; I will not fail you or forsake you" (Joshua 1:5).

Unworthy:    The lie– "I am not worthy of good things. I do not measure up".

> The truth– "Therefore you are no longer a slave, but a son; and if a son, then an heir through God" (Galatians 4:7).

Unlovable:    The lie – "I am not loveable or even likeable. No one will ever love me".

The truth – "For I am convinced that neither death, nor life, nor angels, nor principalities, nor things present, nor things to come, nor powers, nor height, nor depth, nor any other created thing, will be able to separate us from the love of God, which is in Christ Jesus our Lord" (Romans 8:38 -39).

Remember, schemes will always oppose the legitimate gifting and callings of God. Your call and your gifting are very important to God, to the body of Christ and to the world in general. The schemes of the devil are trying to oppose your gifting. The devil wants to keep your gifting covered or distorted in any possible way he can.

Review questions –

What is the scheme of illegitimacy?


Why does Satan use schemes?


What scheme do you see operating in your life?


How do you plan to get victory over your scheme?

# Chapter Six

## The Road Begins Now

It sounds like a cliché, but it literally is one-step at a time. Many times over the course of my ministry, people have come to me for prayer. The most commonly requested prayerI get is, "Dr. Self, please pray for God's will for my life." There is a lot of teaching about finding God's purpose. I think it is critical for everyone to understand the reason why they were created. We have discussed that in this book because it is still a very important topic. However, the truth is, God loves to unfold His purpose before us. The Lord will show us a step to take and then He will wait to see if we will take it. Once we take this step, the Lord will show us the next step. I believe the Lord waits to see if are faithful with what He has put in front of us before He gives us more.

*"He who is faithful in a very little thing is faithful also in much; and he who is unrighteous in a very little thing is unrighteous also in much"* *(Luke 16:10).*

God's principles do not change. If we can be trusted in the small things put before us, God will trust us with large things. If we cannot be trusted with what the Lord has already given us, why will He trust with more? I believe this principle works with our purpose. God wants us to fulfill our purpose, but He also wants us to trust Him and walk with Him every step of the journey. The trust walk is very important. To demonstrate this, the Lord showed me an example of a book. I had a vision of myself picking up the book and glancing at Chapter One, but I immediately wanted to go to the end of the book to see how it turned out. The Lord made it clear to me the only details I would see would be revealed to me one page at time. God wants us to read and live each page of the book, which is a story of our life and purpose. He does not show us the end of the story or even the middle of the story. If we knew how the story was going to turn out, we would not depend on God. He will show you an overall vision, but not all of the specifics. Most of us would be completely overwhelmed if we knew all of God's plans for us. When we think we understand it all, then our tendency is to try to be in control and be completely self-reliant. You will discover your purpose by continuing daily on the path that God has given you. Your overall purpose may not be hard to discover, but the details you need to complete the enormous task in front of you is going to require faith, trust, and surrender. Faith is so important to God that He intentionally leaves out details, therefore causing us to need to trust Him.

Our natural tendency is to want to have everything figured out, planned out, and worked out in advance. This gives us a sense of control and a false sense of security that comes from being in charge. This is why so many people love traditions. Our traditions make everything predictable and, therefore, traditions create comfort. However, as New Testament believers, the Bible clearly tells us we are to be led by the Spirit of God (Romans 8:14). The Holy Spirit, when left in charge, will always do more than we expect. The Bible says that God's ways are not our ways and His thoughts are not our thoughts (Isaiah 55:8); so, why are we surprised when God does things differently? It takes faith and the courage to surrender. Our flesh, ournatural man, does not like it when he is not in control. However, our new man, our spirit-filledman, has been created to be fully surrendered to the will of God, with Him being in control.

Each step can be fun. Just simply taking a step, even one single step in the right direction, can be very rewarding. Most of us tend to be very goal-oriented. Goals can be good things, but they can also be frustrating when not achieved. The journey with God is much different from a goal-orientated mentality. A goal-oriented person is never satisfied until they reach their goal. A person who is concentrating on the journey with God finds new joy and contentment every day.

God wants you to fulfill your purpose, but He wants you to do it by walking with and trusting in Him every day. Your purpose will gradually come into focus as you take step-after-step with the Lord. When Jesus asked the disciples to come and follow Him, He did not tell them where He was taking them and yet they followed Him. The disciples were destined to do great things, but the day that the Lord called them, they simply started the journey with Jesus, one-step at a time. The journey is the important thing. You do not have to wait to feel content. Each step has its own contentment factor. When you take a correct step,an inner peace immediately follows. When you step off the path, things just do not feel right.

"The LORD said to him, 'What is that in your hand?' And he said, 'A staff'" (Exodus4:2). The Lord asked Moses a very simple question. Moses was about to embark on one of the greatest missions in the history of humankind. The Lord started Moses' journey with thequestion: Moses,what have I given you already? Moses had a staff. It did not look like very much, but it is what he had. You know the rest of the story. That staff was an incredible instrument of the Lord used to deliver the children of Israelby performing great miracles.The journey to the Promised Land began with Moses looking at what he had in his hand and taking one-step back toward Egypt to eventually, deliver millions of Hebrew slaves.

The principle is very powerful. God is asking you now, what has He already given you? What possessions or resources do you have to start your journey to your promised land? What divinely appointed people or relationships are already in your life? What skills come easily and naturally to you? In what direction has your history been pointing you? These areimportant questions andonly you can answer them.

Let us look at divinely appointed relationships. Perhaps you have heard the old expression that says people come into your life for a reason, a season, or a lifetime. There are people you will know all the days of your life, butthere are also people who seem to be around only for a season. Perhaps the most important people are the ones therefor you at the bidding of God for a reason. Just as Moses had what he needed to begin his purpose, you also have relationships you need. It is important you discern the people around you and determine who is seeking God's purposes and who is a distraction.

God is not trying to make it hard for you; Heis literally giving you everything you need to make it to your promised land. We need relationships. Our God is a relational God. Relationships benefit us at many levels. I promise you there are people in your life right now sent by God to aid you in your journey to your promised land. These people may not know this is their purpose, but that does not change the truth. God works this way: as you journey toward your promised land, you will always be assisting other people in their journey to their promised land.

Your journey is a discovery process. You have skills and abilities unique to you. As you journey with God and work toward your promised land, you will see more and more how these skills fit the picture perfectly. Most people live and work well beneath their skill level. Each one of us is perfectly designed instruments in the toolbox of God, used to build His kingdom here on Earth.

Maybe your skills are administration and you are visionary. You know how to plan and delegate to make things happen. Perhaps your skills are more with your hands and you are able to fix anything broken. Maybe your primary skill is usingyour mouth. You are a person of many words and the Lord uses you for encouraging counsel. Your skill can literally be your heart and your ability to love unconditionally, no matter what, showing mercy and compassion. You may be discerning, able to tell what is of God and what is not of God. You may have a great mind; you can teach and explain the ways of the Lord. The purpose here is not to do a teaching on the gifts, although we do that very proficiently at the International College of Ministry, but to make this point: you have skills and talents built within you to make it to your personal promised land and to help others reach theirs. The discovery process of this journey with God will make you keenly aware of your personal skills, the people you need, and all the resources God has given you to make it through your journey. When you start taking steps with the Lord, you will find a peace beyond all understanding, as the Apostle Paul described in Philippians. You just need to simply get still, pray, and think about where you are today and what is it the Lord has called you to do, and what you have right now in your possession that you can use start this walk.

As you go through the process of uncovering your purpose, the most important evidence of your divinely created purpose is going to be within your past. Which way is the arrow of your life pointed?Even in our failures and disappointments, we can learn direction. Failure simply means you tried, have courage, have learned something and have probably discovered God had a better way. When you rewind the tape of your life, you will discover a very large prophetic message from God. You see, my friend, the Lord has been speaking to you your whole life. Before you made mistakes, do you remember that little feeling deep down inside you convicting you of what you are about to do?When you intentionally rebelled against God's will for your life, do you remember those constant pricks in your consciousness? Do you remember the frustration when it seemed your way was completely blocked? Do you remember the disappointment when what you wanted to do did not work out? Do you remember being surprised when all of a sudden an answer appeared that you did not think of? All of these things are gigantic clues to the direction the Lord has been pointing you.

In order to journey toward your promised land in a straight and narrow way, it is important we learn the lessons of our past so we do not continue to take unnecessary detours, but simply move straightinto what God has for us.

Review questions –

Do you see God's purpose unfolding for your life? What is the evidence?


In what small things do you need to be faithful?

Who are your divinely appointed relationships?


Is there a primary message from your past that points to your purpose?
What is the message?

# Chapter Seven

## Know Your Gifts and Your Call

Understanding you are created new by God as well as your natural gifts is critical to finding your promised land and your ultimate happiness and satisfaction. I believe there is a lot of confusion about biblical gifts, so what I want to do here is clarify what Scripture says about gifts. There is a clear distinction between our natural, God created abilities, and the supernatural gifts described in Scripture. Who we are and what we have been designed to do is different than the gifts that are implanted into us by the Holy Spirit.Most teaching simply scrambles the message of gifting and causes confusion. You have natural talents and abilities created in you and have been evident in you for your entire life. These abilities and talents can be matured and grown or they can remain immature and polluted. Knowing the reason for and the purpose of your life is very important to finding peace and contentment here on Earth. It is important not only for your personal satisfaction, but also for the benefit of those whom God has assigned to you. The schemes of the enemy have been to keep you from this purpose and to pervert your gifting. As I have said before, Satan cannot defeat God, so he attacks God indirectly through His chosen vessels, us,bytrying to pervert or destroy their purpose in God's plan. Understanding your gifting takes a little education and a lot of common sense. The devil does not want you to know this and will try to hinder you and distract you as you discover yourself and your purpose. It is important that you persevere and press through all the distractions as you discover your reason for existence.

Again the key scripture concerning gifting is "Before I formed you in the womb I knew you, and before you were born I consecrated you; I have appointed you a prophet to the nations" (Jeremiah 1:5). The principle here is even before Jeremiah was born God knew him and had a purpose for him.Since the Lord makes it clear in His Word that He does not change, then it is safe to say the Lord knew you before you were born and appointed you for a purpose. It seems to be a cliché, but the phrase 'you are not an accident' is actually true. I believe strongly that God determines your purpose before you were born. I believe the demonic attacks upon each individual life keep people away from the purpose that God has for them. God is merciful and willing to help us now even though many of us have strayed so far away from our original design.

God created youwith particular talents and skills unique to you. The Lord spoke to me some years ago as a young man struggling with my identity and self-worth. I will never forget the words He spoke to me. He said, "Ray, there is no one greater than you and there is no one less than you because there is only one you." I know that seems like a strange statement, but it meant the world to me. I knew God was saying I did not have to compare myself to anyone else because I was the one and only Ray Self in the universe. Once that thought set in, it made me free because to that point, I believed other people were more talented, more gifted, and more valuable. You remember that was part of my scheme. I believed other people were more worthy than I was.This was a lie of the enemy of God who was trying to keep me suppressed. When I began to accept myself as a unique person and I quit trying to compare myself to other people, I realized I was not better than anyone else, but neither was I less than anyone else. I was simply who I was. It is important for us to be able to accept who we are as God does.

One of the principles in the teaching of boundaries is self-definition. Each one of us needs to be able to define ourselves. By knowing clearly who we are and who we are not, we can learn to accept and love ourselves, and as we do, we are free to give of ourselves to other people. Not clearly knowingwho we are and what we have makes it difficult for us to give and relate to other people in healthy ways. We need to be in relationships with other people. Our God is a relational God and we have to clearly know who we are and accept who we are in order to relate in a healthy way to other people without losing ourselves in another person. We need to have the same unconditional love for ourselves that we tend to show other people.

Understanding your natural gifts and talents and developing an appreciation for them is critical to finding your promised land, peace and satisfaction during this time we have here on Earth. There are gifts that come from God that are supernatural, such as divine healing, prophecy, and words of knowledge, as mentioned in I Corinthians, chapter 12; however, there are other gifts that simply are our natural talents and abilities, that are just as important to understand.

The Bible mentions three categories of gifting. I am not going to cover each category in complete detail in this book, but I want to mention each one for the sake of clarification. The first category is in Ephesians 4:11, "And He gave some as apostles, and some as prophets, and some as evangelists, and some as pastors and teachers." This is what is commonly known as the "five-fold ministry".These divinely appointed gifts or offices given by Christ represent leadership positions in the body of Christ. I do not believe we are naturally born with these gifts. I believe these are ministry leadership appointments from the Lord in order to equip the body of Christ. Sadly, some ministers today want to appoint themselves into these offices as a matter of self-promotion and a false way to build self-esteem. Because of this problem, there has been a tendency to discredit the ones truly called to these offices. It is similar to the problem of TV preachers who are simply in it for the money, which has led to some discrediting of all TV preachers. This is a demonic scheme to hinder the spread of the Gospel.

One thing to be aware of is that Satan never counterfeits anything unless it is valuable. The fact that there are counterfeit five-fold ministers tells me clearly that there are real five-fold ministers. The fact that there are false prophets tells me there must be real prophets. Because there are false apostles speaks to me that there must be real apostles. The point I want to make here is do not fall for the argument that parts of the New Testament concerning gifts were only for the early Church. It is a ridiculous argument that appears when Scripture taken out of context.

Another category of gifting is the gifts mentioned in I Corinthians, chapter 12. These gifts represent the manifestation gifts of the Holy Spirit. Chapter 12 mentions nine different manifestations of the Holy Spirit. I Corinthians 12:8-10 "For to one is given the word of wisdom through the Spirit, and to another the word of knowledge according to the same Spirit; to another faith by the same Spirit, and to another gifts of healing by the one Spirit, and to another the effecting of miracles, and to another prophecy, and to another the distinguishing of spirits, to another various kinds of tongues, and to another the interpretation of tongues."

The Word of God is clear: the Holy Spirit gives these gifts. The Scripture uses the term "manifestation" of the Holy Spirit. This indicates these gifts are evidences of the working of the Holy Spirit in the believer. These gifts are supernatural in their nature and are for the common good of the body, according to verse seven. There is a distinction between a supernatural gift and a natural gift. A supernatural gift is something you cannot do in your own ability or strength. A natural gift is something you can do in your natural ability and strength. Said another way, a supernatural gift is the working of God flowing through you and a natural gift is a gift created in you since birth. An understanding of these gifts and knowing the differences between an office, a calling from God and a supernatural gift from God, is very important.

Mentioned in Romans, chapter 12:6-10 is the third category of gifting commonly known as the motivational gifts. There is a clear difference with these gifts. The motivational gifts are not supernatural gifts but they are not natural talents and abilities either. It is important you understand and know your natural talents and abilities and the proper working of those in order to find your purpose and move into your individual promised land.

*"Since we have gifts that differ according to the grace given to us, each of us is to exercise them accordingly: if prophecy, according to the proportion of his faith; if service, in his serving; or he who teaches, in his teaching; or he who exhorts, in his exhortation; he who gives, with liberality; he who leads, with diligence; he who shows mercy, with cheerfulness." (Romans 12:6-8).*

Mentioned in these verses areseven gifts. Now what makes these gifts unique is they are natural tendencies. What I am going to do in the following paragraphs is describe these gifts and the evidences of these gifts. Each of you reading this should be able to identify primarily with one of these gifts and secondarily with several others. I first learned of this gifting from the book, "Discover Your God-Given Gifts" by Don and Katie Fortune. Their research and information on this subject has been invaluable to me over the years. I want to mention here it is not only important to know your own gifting, but it is equally important to understanding the gifting of those around you. By understanding the gifting of others, you will not try to force your gift on other people but will appreciate the fact that each person is unique and their gifting is just important as yours. This also helps in understanding those around you and assists you in building healthy relationships.

The first gift mentioned is the gift of prophecy accurately translated as a gift of perceiving or the gift of insight. People with this gifting tend to be very blunt and outspoken having an opinion on every topic and are convicted on whatever their opinion is because they believe it with all of their heart. They tend to think in black and white and are very goal conscious. Something is either God's will or it is not God's will and that is the end of the subject for them. They grieve deeply over the sin of other people and are very strict on themselves. Some people refer to them as being very frank. They have a high level of discernment and are usually correct in their opinions. These people can be very valuable because they see the truth and God's will in most every situation.

Now these gifts also have what I referred to as pollution. A pollution of the gift originates when the gift is not fully mature. Pollution can also result when the person is an unbeliever. A typical pollution of the gift of perceiving is they can become critical and judgmental. They so easily see the flaws and instead of praying about it and using wisdom, they become critical. They can show very little mercy and be completely unaware of gray areas or progress because they think a person is in the will of God or not. So the thinking goes, you made it or you have not made it; it does not matter that you are 80% there. However, when a person with this gift becomes aware of the pitfalls and makes an effort to overcome them, this gift can be an extremely valuable tool in the body of Christ.

People who have this gift have a very strong call to intercession. The Lord shows the perceivers truths, not for them to criticize or judge, but normally it is for the purpose of prayer. It is very important for people with this gifting to use God's wisdom on how to apply the truthsthey have seen. I have always said if you simply want to know the truth about something just asked the perceivers. This gift known is as and is symbolic of the eyes of Christ. This gift sees the truth and does not compromise. A great biblical example of this gift is John the Baptist.

The next gift mentioned in Romans, chapter 12 is the gift of serving. This gift may be the easiest one to spot. It represents the hands of Christ. People with this gift are naturally good with their hands. They are very talented with manual functions. Some people with this gift say they can fix anything. I had a friend with this gift some years ago. I asked him if he knew anything about fixing washing machines since my washing machine was broken. He said he had never worked on a washing machine, but he knew without a doubt that he could fix it. That is exactly what he did. This is typical of the gift of serving. People with this gift see practical needs and are very quick to meet them. They are actually very happy when they notice a job and when it is completed. They like short-term jobs – they generally do not like projects that take years to complete. They tend to want to get things done themselves and they want to get it done efficiently. Servers are very happy when they are helping other people. They are great mechanics, carpenters, or electricians or they can simply be a "jack-of-all-trades." They are very vital to the body of Christ and meeting practical needs.

People with this gift tend to be very organized and have a high level of energy. I have a pastor friend who has this gift. Not long ago during the terrible catastrophe in Haiti because of massive earthquakes, he organized a huge relief program for the people of Haiti. He pastors a church in Orlando and because of his connections with churches around the country, he had tents, generators, bulldozers, trucks, and medical supplies sent to Orlando. He then drove all of these donations to Miami, put them on a ship, and made sure the itemsgot to the correct people in Haiti. It was an amazing effort by one man. He organized over $250,000 of relief for that nation. I clearly remember him one Sunday morning talking about the relief effort and he said the words I will not ever forget. He said, "Driving all that stuff to Miami and putting it on a ship was really fun." That stuck with me because I knew he was using his motivational gifts of serving to serve the body of Christ and it was fun for him because he was doing what God created him to do. The gifts work that way.

Servers have some possible pollution, too,just as do the other gifts. A person with a gift of serving not shown appreciation can become very frustrated. A server tends to get frustrated when other people do not appear to enjoy serving the way they do. To do these practical things is natural for the server, but it can be more difficult for people with other giftings. It is important for the server to understand not everybody has the same gift as him or her and God intended it to be that way.

The next gift I want to talk about is the gift of teaching. This gift represents the mind of Christ. People with the gift of teaching love to do research. Facts and word studies are a way of life for them. They tend to have great intellect. God loves to use the teachers to explain the Word of God. A preacher will proclaim the Word of God on Sunday, but a teacher will break it down through word study and explain the Word of God. Teachers tend to have a very even-keeled personality. I call them flat liners. I do not mean this to be critical, it is just they do not get emotional and or have extreme highs or lows; they just seem to keep everything on a level basis. Teachers generally are not happy unless they are teaching. If the teacher does not have a job as a teacher, they will find other ways to teach. They love to hand you books and reading material for you to explore. Since they love to read and study, they naturally figure everybody loves to read and study, which is not necessarily true.

Teachers have to be careful because of their great intellect; they can easily fall into the trap of pride. Their gifting is to explain the Word of God and to impart knowledge to the body of Christ. Pride can be a great obstacle for them, so they must be aware. Teachers actually find word studies and research very enjoyable. They base their life on facts and information. They believe that if you know the truth, and have enough information, you will be free. They normally live their lives according to biblical principles and do not stray. I think all of us know some teachers in our lives.

The next gift mentioned in Romans, chapter 12 is the gift of exhortation, the exhorter, known as the mouth of Christ is a person with many words, has a lot to say, and is typically very encouraging. Exhorter's make great counselors and are very people-oriented. The exhorter loves to encourage people to live victorious. The exhorter typically will take the information from the teacher and will give practical application to the listener. The exhorter lives life according to biblical standards and usually does it in reverse. Typically, they will have an experience and then find it in Scripture. Spotting or should I say hearing the exhorter is easy. If you are in a phone conversation with an exhorter, it may be many minutes before you are able to get a word in the conversation. When called upon to give a testimony, you may want to grab a cup of coffee and relax because an exhorter is going to be a while. Exhorters love to encourage and build up those around them. I love to say, if you are ever feeling depressed,do not call the perceiver because they will simply tell you what you what the problem is and willprobably be correct in their assessment. However, if you want to be encouraged, call the exhorter.

The gift of exhortation, like other gifts, also have possible pollution because they are so eager to speak, they tend to interrupt others. Another problem is they really do not know when to stop talking. I have had exhorters interrupt the class with something they want to say and this can be very disruptive. When the exhorter is counseling(and remember, they do make naturally good counselors), they tended to counsel in the following manner:

1) They will tell their counselee a specific course of action they want them to take.

2) They will give three or four steps they believe will solve the problem.

3) If the counselee does not follow the prescription of the exhorter, eventually the exhorter will cut them off. The thinking is if you are not going to do what I say, why should I counsel you? However, the bottom line is, all of us need to be encouraged, and that is why God created the exhorters.

The next gift mentioned in Romans Chapter 12 is the gift of giving. Givers represent the arms of Christ. You can think of them as the ones who reach out and help others in need. Givers are great managers of money and tend to be very successful in business. They are natural born entrepreneurs. Some say they have the golden thumb, whatever they touch turns to gold. They are very good managers and stewards of the resources God has given them. They understand God is their provision and they are strictly managers of what God has entrusted to them. Givers tend to have wealth. Givers clearly demonstrate the principles of sowing and reaping. The Holy Spirit leads givers in their giving and though many may try to manipulate the giver into giving to a particular ministry, they are not naïve nor are they easy to manipulate.Because God can trust them with His resources and they know how to give, God blesses them financially and in other ways.

Givers make natural evangelists. I had a very wealthy friend who is a giver. He would send himself to very impoverished areas and use his money while there to plant churches and lead people to Christ. A giver loves to give without people knowing about it. They are not looking to please man, but looking to please the Lord. One story that always blesses me when I think about it is about a class I held some years ago. I was teaching for a local Bible college and at that time, the students were required to pay for each course as they took it on the first day of class. The cost of that particular course was $75. There was one pastor there on this cold winter night that came to class but did not have the money to pay. I did not say anything as I have always had a policy of not refusing people because of financial hardship. This man laid his coat and hat down on a chair. The class was an hour and a half long and when class was over, the pastor picked up his hat and $75 fell out of it. Naturally, he was very blessed and surprised. I knew someone with the gift of giving placed money within his hat and did not want anyone to know who did it, which is typical of the gift of giving. Another story that demonstrates this motivational gift very clearly was some years ago when I was in Bible College. It was time to graduate and I was short $300 on my tuition. My friend Jim invited me to go to breakfast with him. Jim and I were just having a pleasant conversation when he reached in his pocket and he said the Lord told him to give this to me. He pulled out three $100 bills and handed them to me. It was the exact amount of my tuition bill. I had not told him about my money situation. Jim was operating in his motivational gift. I have never forgotten it.

Givers also have some pollution that they need to be aware of. Some givers will use their money to get out of work. For instance, it may be a workday at the church and it is time to repaint the building. The giver may buy the paint, but not lift a brush. On the other hand, the giver may make a generous gift to the church to replace the carpet in the sanctuary, but specify that his money is to buy only a green carpet. The giver must be careful not to fall into these traps.

The next gift, depending on the version of the Bible you are reading, is administration also known as the shoulders of Christ. People with this gift shoulder responsibility and are visionaries. Unlike the servers who tend to see short-term jobs and want to get it done quickly, the administrators are able to see long-term vision. They love working toward goals. They love delegating and doing anything causing the goal to be achieved. They despise red tape and/or delays and are simply happy when they are working toward their vision or the vision given them. They do not care about getting credit for the job; they just want to see the job taken care of. They are people-oriented and are normally great communicators. They are not maintainers or settlers; they are pioneers.

In other words, they find their joy in the journey toward the goal, but once achieved, they do not want to stop there. They want to start toward another goal. The administrator understands working under authority, but if no clear authority exists, they will take the lead. They are great planners and strategists, but they have to be careful not to misuse people or take advantage of people just to accomplish their goal. They must also be careful not to neglect their own families because of their goal-focus. A good biblical example of this gift would be Joseph, who had a long-term strategy for helping Egypt with an upcoming famine. Administrators can carry great burdens and are valuable assets to the body of Christ. Many of the biblical apostles had this motivational gifting.

The last, but most given gift, is a gift of compassion. This gift represents the heart of Christ. Some studies show this gift represents about 35% of the body of Christ. I believe the reason for this is the need for compassion. People with this gift are tenderhearted and have a great capacity to show love and mercy. They will trust people until proven wrong. Some people mistakenly think people with compassion are doormats and that is far from the truth. People with this gift are very strong and choose to show mercy and forgiveness, even when it is very difficult to do so. When they love, they love with all their hearts. When they feel, they feel with all their hearts. People with this gift can literally feel the atmosphere of a room. They can also deeply sense the inner pain of people. It is easy for people with this gift to empathize because they can honestly say, "I feel you."

An unusual part of this gifting is people with the gift of compassion can easily discern hypocrisy. The person with the gift of compassion picks it up immediately if the person speaking to them is not sincere. People with this gift have a natural heart toward the disadvantaged. Compassionate people cannot stand injustice. If it is unfair, they will stand up and fight. People with this gift are very sensitive and can be hurt very easily. Their hearts can be deeply wounded therefore need to be protected. Compassion-gifted people love to love. They have this endless well of love stored inside of them waiting to spill over.

As with other gifts, there are problems or pollution to be aware of with this gift. Because of the pain in their heart for other people, those with this gift can be prone to depression and addictions.Especially in dealing with the opposite sex, people with this gift have to be careful that their Godly love not be mistakenfor another type of love.

Sometimes people with this gift tend to be like volcanoes. They can store up the pain caused by circumstances or other people takingmany hits before finally having had enough. When a person with the gift of compassion has had enough, watch out! They actually become the opposite of compassion. They can fly into an absolute fit of rage. It takes a lot for them to get to that point, but they need to be aware that this is a possibility.

The gift of compassion can be called the gift of love and it is a great gift, even if it can be a painful gift. Jesus was moved by compassion. *"When the Lord saw her, He felt compassion for her, and said to her, 'Do not weep'"* (Luke 7:13).

Your individual call from the Lord will involve your gifting. Many people ask me to pray for God's will for their lives. I do not think God's will is a big secret that He wants to hide from us. I think God is trying to communicate to us clearly, what He has called us to do. What you have been called to do I believe you will naturally do well. However, God will also supernaturally empower you with His strength. Your call from God will always be in more than you can do naturally. If your call can be accomplished in your own strength, then who needs God? All credit would go to you and God would not be pleased. Your purpose and call will be unique. It will evolve and unfold gradually before you.

I thinkthat sometimes we limit ourselves by thinking our call from God has to be church ministry.Your calling could be to a church ministry, but God is even bigger than that. Your call, along with your physical skills and verbal ability, could involve business, your family, and your community. Your gifts, as we have just discussed in this chapter, are evidences of your call. Finding your purpose and moving into it is where you will find your satisfaction and peace. If you are presently feeling frustrated and a little dissatisfied, perhaps you are out of your purpose.

In my life, I drifted far away, from what God called me to do. However, no matter how far away you are from your call, God is gracious and merciful to help you get back on the right track. Your first step may be to discover how to find your way back to what God has called you to do. God is more than able and willing to help you get back to where you belong. You can choose to continue the way you are going, but it is not God's will for you and you will never find true happiness there. Remember, God is not an enabler, so He is not going to enable you to move in a direction He did not call you to. If you are outside of His purpose and His will, your success is going to be limited. By being in the will of God, your success and your potential arelimitless. Pray for God to make it clear to you His purpose. It is a prayer that He loves to answer.

One obvious way to discover your purpose is to look at what the devil is trying to keep you away from. I have often said the devil works in opposites. If you are to lead, Satan will try to make you think you are incapable. If you are to teach, he will try to convince you that you are not very smart. If you are to preach, he may try to convince you nobody wants to hear you. If you are to write, the devil may try to convince you nobody would want to read your words. If you are calledto business, he may try to convince you that your business idea will never work. In other words, you can use Satan's schemes and weapons to help determine your call.

Finally, the Bible is very clear about what we should do when we need wisdom. James 6 says, "But if any of you lacks wisdom, let him ask of God, who gives to all generously and without reproach, and it will be given to him. But he must ask in faith without any doubting, for the one who doubts, is like the surf of the sea, driven and tossed by the wind."

Review questions:

Why it is important to understand gifts as described in Scripture?

What are the three categories of gifts and who gives them?

How do the motivational gifts shape our personality?

How does your primary motivational gift relate to your purpose?

# Chapter Eight

## Happiness and Satisfaction

There is an old Rolling Stones song called "Satisfaction." One of the lyrics in the song goes something like this – "I can't get no, satisfaction, but I tried and I tried and I tried." I am sure Mick Jagger did not intend his song to be a song dealing with psychological problems, but actually,there is so much truth in this lyric that it is amazing. I believe the world in general has been in a constant search to find satisfaction. The search involves looking for satisfaction in many ways and forms. Some look for satisfaction in money. Some look for satisfaction in worldly success. The problem is always the same; it goes back to the Rolling Stones song lyric –"I can't get no, satisfaction."

The trap, as I mentioned earlier, is the trap of never enough. In my personal life,I was in this trap for many years. I believed deeply that if I was successful in business I would be happy and satisfied. I have always had a love for boats, especially sailboats. I purchased my first sailboat in the 70's. It was a 16-foot sailboat called a Laser. After some time, I believed I would be much happier with the larger boat, so I purchased a 21-foot San Juan sailboat. I loved that boat and had a lot of fun on it, but I believed I would be happier if I had a larger boat. So a few years later, I purchased a Ranger 26-foot sailboat. Each one of these boats was a lot of fun, but I always had a feeling that I needed something more. The story goes on and I purchased a 35-foot Pearson sailboat. Surely, now I would have found the peace that I long for. Unfortunately, I was in the trap of never enough. One day a friend was talking to me and she said something that changed my life. She said, "Ray, things do not make you happy." That statement hit me hard. I had looked for happiness in many things. I thought I could find happiness in a bigger boat. I thought I could find happiness by owning my own business (I actually started five different corporations). I thought I could find happiness by driving a Cadillac and by being the head of my own company. I looked for happiness in a variety of ways, but that statement by a friend literally changed my life. If things would not make me happy what would make me happy? I pondered that question for a long time. Eventually, I came to realize things can be fun or enjoyable, but they do not bring peace and happiness. Somewhere was a peace that I was looking for and a satisfaction that I was longing for and I wanted it desperately.

I read in Scripture that God could give me a peace that passes all understanding. I began to realize there was a peace beyond human or even the world's understanding and it can only come from God. I knew if I did not find that peace, I would continually strive to look in all the wrong directions and I would be continually wasting my life.

I do not believe my story is much different from yours. I think the principles are solid and the trap is real. The best way to avoid a trap is to be aware of where the trap is and what it looks like. I have described my trap only in part. I think most people spend much of their lives in a vain search for satisfaction. You see, my friend, happiness is like a roller coaster ride – it goes up and down, depending on the circumstance. God's peace and satisfaction remain deep inside and can bring us fulfillment every day.

I had some key moments in my life that changed my search for happiness. I was like most, constantly looking for ways to be happy, but it was an incredibly rocky road. There were several times in my past that my life took a dramatic change. One pivotal moment was when I was in Bible College. The president of the college was a preacher preaching in a revival in a small town in Arkansas. I was simply a student working on my degree. I entered Bible College late in life because I did not find my call or purpose until I was around 44-years old. The Bible College was in Memphis Tennessee and my instructor, who was also the college president, had been driving every evening to a small town in eastern Arkansas to preach in a revival that had been going on for weeks. This revival was truly a move of God with people being saved, and healed. The local drug dealer came to the revival one night, laid all his drug paraphernalia on the altar, and surrendered his life to the Lord.

One day in class, my instructor told me he could not preach that night at the revival and asked me to go in his place. I was shocked and very nervous. I worked up my courage and drove to the small town in Arkansas. The church was small, hot, and crowded. People in the audience were optimistic because they had been witnessing the Lord doing miraculous things for the last several weeks. After the music played and the introduction, I stood up to preach. I do not remember exactly what I preached about, but I do remember the audience responding to me. I remember vividly the incredible sense of satisfaction that I had never felt before. Finally, I had found peace. I had walked into my purpose and it really felt good! I preached the word of God and I witnessed the Lord move powerfully throughout the church. I think what actually happened was there was a revival inside of me as I began to discover my purpose.

There are many stories to tell concerning peace and happiness. Let me share one more key moment in my life to demonstrate a point. On another occasion, my college professor asked me to teach a class on the motivational gifts at another campus, which was in a local church. I taught the class the best that I could. I do not remember anything being very special about my teaching, but what changed my life was what happened after my teaching. The pastor of that church came up to me after class and said, "Ray, you are really a good teacher." I remember being surprised at those words. This was a well-known pastor and he had just told me that I was a good teacher. Now, this may not sound like anything to you, but at this point in my life, I was just beginning to discover my purpose. This the first time I taught anything formally as a minister. I had no idea that I was good at it. Sometimes, it truly takes someone with an objective viewpoint to identify your gifting. I remember those words very clearly, because I remember as I was teaching it felt normal and right and I had a sense of peace as I was doing it. The affirmation of that pastor opened up my eyes to see another part of my calling.

Now when I look back on my life working in sales and marketing, I can see evidence of this. There were times in the business world that I would make a sales presentation to a group of people and I seemed to be very good at it. The truth is that God did not want me to sell material things. He wanted me to sell the truth of the gospel of Jesus Christ. I was in the appliance and electronics business. I was just selling things to make money. In actuality, it was a twisted version of my purpose.

I read recently on the Internet the following: Happiness is the only true measure of personal success. Making other people happy is the highest expression of success, but it is almost impossible to make others happy if you are not happy yourself (Inc.com). It is interesting that even the worldview seems to understand the relationship between real success and happiness. I think,however, as Christians we should seek something more than happiness. We should seek the true peace and inner joy that can only come from one source – God working through His Holy Spirit.

The point here is, finding and doing what you were designed will bring peace and satisfaction. It is not true what Mick Jaggar sang – satisfaction can be found.

*"These things I have spoken to you so that My joy may be in you, and that your joy may be made full." (John 15:11).*

Our goal should be to have the peace and joy that never leaves. There is a peace and a joy that literally can be within your spirit or down deep in your heart and can be there every day. It does not come from things or from circumstance, but instead it comes supernaturally from the Creator when you are in His will and led by His Spirit following His path. Our natural tendency, because we live in a fallen world and we still have fleshly fallen tendencies, is to try to find peace, joy, and satisfaction in whatever this life can offer through material things, other people, success, money, achievement, etc. This peace or happiness that comes from our society is fleeting, at best. It changes like the wind and is never permanent. My desire is for you to have that peace within your heart, peace that is always there no matter what.

Many things make me happy. I love to see a beautiful sunrise. I love nature and God created beauty. I live in Central Florida where there are lakes, springs, and tropical flowers everywhere and I feel happy when I look at them. I get happy when my favorite football team wins. I get happy when I can drive a golf ball 300 yards and have it land in the fairway. I get happy at the sound of my wife's voice. I get happy when I see my kids in Memphis Tennessee. In other words, many things that make me happy and I do not discount that, but there is a peace and a joy that the Lord wants us to have down inside our hearts. If this peace is not within us, we will constantly be searching, striving, and trying in a continuously failing attempt to obtain it.

*"And the peace of God, which surpasses all comprehension, will guard your hearts and your minds in Christ Jesus" (Philippians 4:7).*

Doing what you were created to do will bring you peace, you will have that ever-elusive sense of satisfaction when you are doing or moving toward what you were created to do. There is another key moment in my life, which I briefly mentioned earlier. In the mid to late 80's, my life had become a mess. It is a long and painful story and actually, it is unbelievable, but true. My marriage was failing terribly. The pain of betrayal was incredibly hard to bear. In the midst of this, my stepson had gotten heavily involved in drugs and demonic activities. About the same time, a former business partner falsely accused me of racketeering and sued me for one million dollars. I had to fight the accusation in federal court, which eventually was thrown out. Praise God! However, the stress, and strain of fighting that lie was horrible. I found out my secretary had not been paying payroll taxes, so the Internal Revenue Service decided to come hard after me, personally. There are more details of the story, but I guess you can see my life was a wreck.

One day my mother, who is a wonderful Christian woman, told me about a friend of hers from church named John who prayed for people at his home. My mother went on to tell me that there had been several miraculous healings taken place in this man's living room. For some unknown reason, in my heart I felt I really wanted to meet this man. My mother set up a meeting. I will never forget what happened next. I walked into his home and John met me. Immediately he asked me a question I had never heard before. He said, "Ray, have you ever heard of the baptism of the Holy Spirit." I grew up in a Southern Baptist church and was not taught about the baptism of the Holy Spirit. I told John that I did not understand. He then took me to Scripture and showed me some very clear passages. The first one he showed me was Acts1:5, "...for John baptized with water, but you will be baptized with the Holy Spirit not many days from now." Then he showed me Acts 1:8, "...but you will receive power when the Holy Spirit has come upon you; and you shall be My witnesses both in Jerusalem, and in all Judea and Samaria, and even to the remotest part of the earth." He definitely had my attention because I felt that was the reason for me being at his home, even though I did not know what it was. John then took me to Acts8:14-17, "Now when the apostles in Jerusalem heard that Samaria had received the word of God, they sent them Peter, and John, who came down and prayed for them that they might receive the Holy Spirit. For He had not yet fallen upon any of them; they had simply been baptized in the name of the Lord Jesus. Then they began laying their hands on them, and they were receiving the Holy Spirit."

I began to realize that the Lord had something else for me that night. John did not stop there, he took me also to Acts, chapter 10 where Peter was preaching and the Holy Spirit fell upon those with whom he was talking. However, perhaps the Scripture that sealed the deal for me was Acts 19:2, "He said to them, "Did you receive the Holy Spirit when you believed?" And they said to him, "No, we have not even heard whether there is a Holy Spirit."In addition,Acts19:6, "And when Paul had laid his hands upon them, the Holy Spirit came on them, and they began speaking with tongues and prophesying."

I realized that I was a Christian, but God had more for me. Then, I had a rather silly thought. I felt like, as a Christian up to this point, I was enjoying chocolate cake but now I had found the icing. John asked me if I was ready to receive this baptism and I said yes. He then asked me a series of questions about my past and asked me to repent of previous sins. After that, John had me sit in a chair and he put his hand on my shoulder. I do not remember the exact words he prayed, but it was something like this, "Lord Jesus, I ask now you come and baptized my brother Ray with the

Holy Spirit." I remember it was not a lengthy prayer but immediately I began to feel and sense things I had never felt before in my life. I sat there quietly in this chair and I had a strange feeling as if someone was pouring warm oil over me. I thought to myself, well this certainly is strange but it really does feel good. I then began to feel this incredible sense of peace in my body. It was not in the mind; it was in my spirit and in my heart. This was the first peace I had felt in a long time. My life was a complete mess, but I was sitting in this chair and I felt a total peace throughout my body. The next thing I remember is I had this sense of unconditional love coming down from above. I do not know exactly how to describe this, but I just felt totally loved and it felt very good. As I continued to sit there with my eyes closed, I remember clearly sensing this love was not ordinary, but very powerful. I had a sense something very powerful was flowing over me and in me.

I know now what took place. It was the Holy Spirit filling me and empowering me. It was what the Scripture calls the baptism of the Holy Spirit. I was saved in 1961 and I was baptized with the Holy Spirit in 1986. Some mistakenly tell you that you get baptized with the Holy Spirit the moment you are saved. I will tell you that is not necessarily true. In Scripture and especially in Acts chapter 8, you clearly see people who were saved and accepted Jesus Christ as Savior and then later received the baptism of the Holy Spirit. The Holy Spirit does the work in us to save us and cause us to be born again and adopted children of God, but He does another work called the baptism of the Holy Spirit that gives us power to serve and be a witness for the Lord.

*"...but you will receive power when the Holy Spirit has come upon you"* *(Act 1:8).*

*"And behold, I am sending forth the promise of My Father upon you; but you are to stay in the city until you are clothed with power from on high"* *(Luke 24:49).*

In order to do what God is calling you to do and to find peace and satisfaction, we need the help of the Holy Spirit. He can fill you with His power and can truly give you peace that passes anything the world has to offer. That is what happened to me, and millions of Christians worldwide. Do not let any well-meaning Christians and traditional churches tell you this stuff is not for today and the Bible is not true or it is partially true. We cannot pick, and choose which parts of the Bible are true and not true. I know what the Bible says and I have experienced it. If you have not been baptized with the Holy Spirit, you should seek that now or find a spirit filled church that understands this promise and ask them to pray for you, that you may be baptized with the Holy Spirit. In order to possess your promised land and apply peace and satisfaction to your life, you will need this power from above dwelling within you to accomplish what God has for you.

Happiness and peace come by fulfilling your God given purpose and that requires more power than we contain ourselves. Our potential is very large. Our God is even larger. My question to you is, what are you doing now in comparison to the potential God has put within you? What is your level of peace and satisfaction compared to the peace and satisfaction that God has for you? Are you on the road to your promised land and are you able to defeat the enemies along the way? Can you see it on the horizon or are you still wandering in your own personal wilderness?

Review questions –

Are you searching for happiness? Have you been looking in the wrong direction? What do you believe will bring you peace and happiness?

What were you doing in your past when you felt happy and content?

What is the baptism of the Holy Spirit and why is it important?

Are you living to your potential? What is your potential?

# Part Two

# Your Promised Land

## Chapter Nine

## The Four Stages of Your Promised Land

*"O Israel, you should listen and be careful to do it, that it may be well with you and that you may multiply greatly, just as the LORD, the God of your fathers, has promised you, in a land flowing with milk and honey"* *(Deuteronomy 6:3).*

What is a promised land? The Promised Land was designed specifically for you even before you were born, where God is giving you authority to accomplish His will. To me it is a place including people, specific circumstances, and geographic conditions. It is a place in life promised and given by God and containsall you and those around you need to live a blessed life. It is a place where you feel satisfied, find contentment, and prosper. It is a place figuratively flowing with milk and honey.

Your life has been a journey. This journey contained many roads and byways. Some of the roads headed in the right direction, but many of them headed in the wrong direction. Some of the roads were blocked, but some of the roads seemed to go on and on even though we headed the wrong way. Many times, we came to an intersection and had choices to make. Some of the choices were good and some were bad. The amazing thing about God is He has an incredible way to make bad choices eventually work for our good.

*"And we know that God causes all things to work together for good to those who love God, to those who are called according to His purpose"* *(Romans 8:28).*

That Scripture is the grace of God working in our lives. God knows we will make bad choices and decisions not in His will, but through His grace, He can make everything come out the way He wants it to in the end. Everyone's personal life is a culmination of all of their choices they have made. Where I am today is a result of God's will working through a combination of all of the choices I have made in my life. I have made some very bad choices and I have made some good choices. Somehow, through His grace, the power of God got me to my promised land. I could have gotten here much quicker if it were not for the bad choices, but I am here. This is God's grace and determination to get His will donein my life, because it's not just about me. It is also about the people God has assigned to me.

The great news is that your promised land is better than you could ever imagine. That is the way God works, He always does bigger, better and greater things in our lives than we could ever think of. In this way,there is no doubt as to who gets the glory.

*"Now to Him who is able to do far more abundantly beyond all that we ask orthink, according to the power that works within us, to Him be the glory in the church and inChrist Jesus to all generations forever and ever. Amen" (Eph.3:20-21).*

A promised land is a place God has designed for you and promised you. It is where He wants you to be. It is where God wants to bless you and prosper you. It is also a place of authority. Your promised land is a place God has given you authority to do great things in His name and although you will have many battles, it is a place God has promised you will always be victorious. The journey to this place has been difficult for many people and because of the hindrances of the devil, this journey is especially difficult for people who do not understand the principles of spiritual warfare and the power and authority of the Name above all names, Jesus.

I want to emphasize here, your promised land is not always a different city or state. A promised land is simply working in and living in the will and purpose of God for your life. Just to do that may require a physical move, but your promised land and can be right where you are. You can be in the middle of your promised land, but not be reaping the benefits of it because you are in a form of disobedience to your purpose, even though you are in the right place.

Let me give this example. Perhaps you have been attending a church in your community for some time and every Sunday you sit in the midst of the congregation and enjoy the music and the message. This church could be part of your promised land, but you are not reaping the benefits. You know in your heart that God wants you to assist or lead in a ministry of the church, but instead of doing that, you become one of the many anonymous faces sitting in the audience Sunday after Sunday. God has a divine purpose for you being in that church, but you have not stepped up to the plate. You may be heavily involved in your job and family, so much so you could be thinking, "How could I have time to do anything else?" You must understand when you start acting in obedience to the purpose of your life, God will bless every area of your life. As I have written earlier in this book, Satan wants desperately to keep you away from the will of God for your life. One of most effective ways he accomplishes his scheme against you is simply by keeping you busy. We must become aware of this and be willing to fight and press through the obstacles to do what God has called us to do.

There is a lot at stake in your personal promised land. Your own contentment and satisfaction is at stake, but more importantly, there are many people that will benefit from your purpose. Our God is a God of love; He loves His people deeply. Whatever it is you are called to do, it will always benefit other people. If a person refuses to accept his promised land, this is actually an act of selfishness. Your promised land is an attitude of faith and a willingness to surrender to God's will for your life. Your promised land is a place where God wants you to be blessed so you can, in turn, be a blessing to others.

I cannot tell you exactly where your promised land is or exactly what your promised land looks like, but I do clearly understandthe benefits of it. I know if every Christian in America would get into the place God has called them and do what God has called them to do, our country would be a much better place. It is one of those situations where you have everything to gain and nothing to lose. It is a situation you may have to fight for and even adjust to, but it is God's will for your life. I know that the body of Christ has been crippled by divisions and by the fact that most of the work being done is done by a minorityof leaders. If each person in the body of Christ would operate in the purpose for which he or she were designed, the body of Christ would be incredibly more powerful and more influential than we could ever imagine.

I think it is sad that many churches have become a spectator sport or an entertaining theatrical production with a studio audience. They seem to be a place people want to go to sit with the crowd and watch the show. Many times in the past, I have been one of those spectators, just watching the show. As idle, passive spectators, much of God's will and purpose for our lives is simply wasting away. We can be spectators rather than participants for manythings in our lives. Are you a person who is simply watching the game when you are called to be a player? This is a question that only you can answer. An important point to remember is that there is no condemnation for those in Christ Jesus (Romans 8:21). I am not trying to condemn you or place guilt on you, but I am hoping the Holy Spirit will convict your heart and lead you into the place God has called you.

Review Questions –

In the context of this book, what is a promised land?

What does your personal promised land look like?

Why is it important for you to be living and operating in your personal promised land?

What is the Holy Spirit convicting you to do about your purpose?

# Chapter Ten

## Getting There

The first stage is getting to it. In previous chapters in this book, we have talked about the many hindrances and obstacles that get in the way of our journey to our promised land. We have discussed the importance of removing these hindrances and prayerfully you are free of anyone or anything slowing you down. The most important thing about your promised land is you must get to it. You need to realize the schemes of Satan are in place to stop you from getting to your promised land. This should also be a signal to you that for you to be in your promised land is God's will and that is why the devil has fought so hard and so long to keep you away from it.

Getting to the Promised Land reminds me of the most difficult obstacle concerning physical exercise. All of us know we need to get plenty of exercise to keep our bodies healthy. Many people say the most challenging obstacle about exercise is the front door to the gym. You must first get to the door and go through the door before you can do any type of fitness center exercises. Completing the journey to the place the Lord has for you can be the greatest challenge of all. The purpose of this book is to help many people overcome those challenges.

We should be encouraged and know the Lord has given us power and authority to conquer. The Lord wants us to get to our own individual promised land. The Lord wants His army in place, but not only 'in place' but in the right place. There is a story in the Bible that demonstrates this very clearly. The story is told in 2 Chronicles, chapter 20. King Jehoshaphat was the king of Judah. Three nations gathered to make war against him and his country. King Jehoshaphat was very afraid and he sought the Lord. He had the whole country pray and fast because of the crisis at hand; thevery future of his nation was at stake. The king called out to the Lord, "O our God, will You not judge them? For we are powerless before this great multitude who are coming against us; nor do we know what to do, but our eyes are on You" (2 Chronicles 20:12). All the people of Judah had gathered to pray when all of a sudden the spirit of the Lord came upon a man called Jahaziel. This man was a complete unknown, but he had the spirit of the Lord on him. He said, "Listen, all Judah and the inhabitants of Jerusalem and King Jehoshaphat: thus says the LORD to you, 'Do not fear or be dismayed because of this great multitude, for the battle is not yours but God's'"(v.15). The Lord was offering His people comfort and letting them know that He understood their struggle and their fear, but at the same time He was with them.

The Bible says God has not changed. I want you to know the Lord is with you and He understands your fears and your struggles. What appear to be overwhelming forces that seem to be coming against you is not a problem for our God. In this story, there is a tremendous crisis and the people know the only thing they can do is to call on the Lord. The interesting part of the story is the Lord's instructions to the people of Judah.

2 Chronicles 20:16-17says, "Tomorrow go down against them. Behold, they will come up by the ascent of Ziz, and you will find them at the end of the valley in front of the wilderness of Jeruel. 'You need not fight in this battle; station yourselves, stand and see the salvation of the LORD on your behalf, O Judah and Jerusalem.' Do not fear or be dismayed; tomorrow go out to face them, for the LORD is with you."

The Lord tells the people of Judah to go to a certain place. The Lord is very specific about this place and time. Note in the above scripture, He says the time is tomorrow and the place is the end of the valley by the ascent of Ziz. The instructions are to go there and simply stand. In this exact place and time, the Lord promised that the nation of Judah would be saved. In this place, the Lord promises there will be a victory. Note in this scripture, there was a particular place the Lord wanted to put His people in order to save them. He asked them to go to the end of the valley, a particular valley, and stand still. The story goes on and tells how the people went to the end of the valley of Ziz and there they began to praise and worship God. This was more than the Lord had asked them to do, but praise and worship is always appropriate. The people were obedient to God and had placed themselves where the Lord had asked them to be and there they had victory.

There are great principles we can learn from this story. Hearing the voice of God and following His instructionsarecritical to success. Many of us like to go wherever we want to go, but that is not where we will necessarily see the victory the Lord promised. The Lord has a specific place He wants us to be and place He wants us to stand in order to see His victory. Are you in the place the Lord has asked you to be? The Lord wants all of us to be in our promised land. It is the place of peace, contentment, prosperity and it is the place we will see the victory of God in our lives.

Abraham had to go to another land to receive his promise. The entire nation of Israel had to leave one country and go to another to receive their promise. I am not saying God wants you to leave and go to another state or country or nation. Sometimes your promised land is right in front of your nose. Sometimes the Promised Land is a change in your attitude and your belief systems. The Promised Land can be when you start acting in obedienceby living in and doing your purpose even where you are. However, my experience tells me sometimes the place Godcalled you can be completely different from where you are. Rest assured; God is not going to send you to a place you will not like. Your promised land will be enjoyable for you and it will actually lighten your burden.

Some time ago, I had a vision of a chess game where I saw a very large chessboard with God's hand strategically moving the pieces of the chessboard into different positions as He was forming His strategy for victory. I saw that the various pieces on the chessboard represented us and God was strategically placing us where He wanted us to be, in and with whom He wanted us to be. I saw God had a grand strategy and it was important for each Christian to cooperate and allow God to place him or her where He needed them to be. I realized this was a very serious game, part of a large cosmic battle. Moreover, whether we like it or not, we are the chesspieces.

A large part of God's strategy to conquer is our relationships. Our God is very interested in relationships. First, He wants a relationship with us, but secondly, He wants us to have healthy relationships with those around us. I believe God arranges things divinely, through circumstances, to get us in correct relationships. I also believe Satan tries to counter these moves of God with counterfeit relationships. It is up to us to discern what relationship is from God and what relationships are not. Relationships can be very helpful, but relationships, as we all know, can also be very harmful. It is important for us to surround ourselves with people who understand the will of God for our lives.

As I mentioned earlier in the book, when you make a move to a different place or position in your life, there will be two groups of people. There will be those who understand and support you and there will be those who will criticize you. Most people criticize because of low self-esteem and feeling threatened by other's success. However, please understand, your true friends are those who understand the will of God for your life and will help and support you in God's purpose for you.It is painful to realize there are relationships we must leave behind, but the good news is that our God is a God of redemption. Sometimes your enemies, as Jesus warned us, can be members of your own household. Sometimes your enemies will be close friends. Satan loves to use people close to us to hinder us, because people close to us carry a large amount of significance. We care about what they think and about what they say. We do not care too much, what a stranger says, but we care deeply about what a person we love says. So if the devil can use someone close to us to hinder us or distract us, he certainly will. History makes it clear that is exactly what he does. I have family members who have never supported me, encouraged me, or really cared about what I do, which has been painful, but God has redeemed that by bringing me new family here in Central Florida who do support me. I have brothers and sisters in Christ, who support me, encourage me, pray for me, and understand what God is trying to do through me. They are my redemptive family. My new brothers and sisters in Florida are a big part of my restoration. God will do the same for you.

When it is time to conquer your promised land, you will need people who are in agreement with you and understand your heart and your vision. You need people in your life that will be to you as Jesus Christ. They will love you unconditionally, but they will also tell you the truth when you need to hear it. Always be aware that Satan will continually try to bring people into your life to distract you from God's purposes. The gift of discernment is a very reliable tool in determining what is of God and what is not. I urge you to simply pray and say, "Lord, help me to discern what is of You."

Over the years, I have witnessed the call of God on many people. He has asked them to move to a different place in life. It could be a call to move from a particular church to another ministry. It could be a call to a different career or a different education. It could be a call to missions or volunteer work. Whatever the call, whatever the Lord is asking us to do; I find one of the greatest enemies is comfort. We as humans love our comfort. Familiarity is very comfortable. It is amazing how long people will stay in the wrong place because it is familiar to them. Even a miserable place can be comfortable because it is so familiar. Routine is comfortable because it is predictable and contains no surprises. It is much the same way with some traditions. Change can be uncomfortable so, naturally, many people resist it.

When God desires for a person to make a move, I have observed the Lord make people uncomfortable in situations that used to be extremely comfortable for them. I believe this is the mercy of God. The Lord knows it is hard for us to move out of the familiar and comfortable, so sometimes He will muddy our waters until we are ready to let go and swim in new streams. I have watched people go into intense spiritual warfare when things get difficult, trying to cast out demons and rebuke the enemy when it was simply the Lord, who wanted them to make a change. If you are in a situation, where you have prayed and prayed for the hard place to be easier, or the rocky road to be flatter, maybe it is the Lord trying to tell you, it is time to go.

Another obstacle in moving to where the Lord wants you to be is what I call personal permission. Sometimes people simply do not give themselves permission to make a change. Some adults seek outside approval and confirmation before making a change. The truth is, all they have to do is tell them it is okay and then they just need to do it. As adults, we do not always have to have permission from other people. An adult will take responsibility by listening to his or her own heart and then do what is right. Adults know how to give themselves permission to make a change. Some people do not tell themselves it is okay to make a change because of fear of disapproval. A mature Christian will care deeply about the concerns of others, but will obey God first, and foremost. A mature Christian knows how to be accountable to authority, but responsible for them.

My journey to my promised land is an interesting story. I was pastoring a small but growing church in North Mississippi near Tennessee. The church had a very strong anointing. During every service, the power of God was very evident. It was common for people to drive over four hours to come to one of our services. At our Sunday evening services, we would get many visitors from other churches who simply needed a touch from the Lord. It was a glorious time in the ministry. In addition to pastoring this church, I was also a director for several satellite campuses of a Florida-based seminary. Little did I know, my training with this Florida seminary was a key to the future that God had for me. The ministry was doing very well for a season and for that particular promised land, but the Lord was calling me to a new land. The call was to Central Florida, an area I had never considered.

Unfortunately, some years before, I had experienced a very painful divorce and had pretty much resigned myself to be a single man serving God the best I could. However, the Lord had a surprise for me. It was an incredible blessing in the form of a beautiful wife. I truly experienced the fact that the Lord will do exceedingly and abundantly more than we could ever think or ask for. My wife lived in Orlando, Florida and I lived in North Mississippi. For the first year and a half of our marriage, we would spend a week in North Mississippi, a week apart, a week in Orlando and then another week apart. We were able to maintain this for a year and a half, but I knew in my heart that a move was necessary. My first and most obvious thought was my wife would move to North Mississippi. My wife prayed and was willing to do that, but the Lord spoke to me. Eventually, I knew in my heart the Lord had a new promised land for me and it was in Central Florida. This was a very difficult decision I did not take lightly because all of my family and friends were in North Mississippi and West Tennessee. I had lived in that area for all of my 56 years; so, this was a gigantic decision. I obeyed God, and laid down my ministry and moved to Central Florida to start over in my new promised land.

Objectively, it seemed like a crazy move. I had a very strong ministry doing great things for the Lord and I had family, friends, and valuable contacts where I was. However, I made the move anyway because I believed in my heart this is what the Lord called me to do.

I made the move and I found myself in a strange land. Please understand I am a traditional southern gentleman. I still say yes ma'am, no sir, and I hold the door open for the ladies. I do not take a seat until the lady has been seated first. I believe in chivalry, good manners, politeness, and hospitality, all of which were part of the Southern culture. When I arrived in Central Florida, I discovered it was not a Southern culture at all. Most of the people in the Orlando area were from the North. Now I am not opposed to people from the North, but the culture is definitely different, so I had some adjusting to do in my new promised land. I moved into a home with my wife and shortly afterwards was introduced to a local pastor. It was a divine introduction. I really liked him. He was very prophetic and very serious about the Lord, but at the same time, he also knew how to have fun and he was really a funny person. I am like that as well. My wife and I visited his church, which was not close to our home and again God surprised me. We walked through the door one Sunday morning and literally within 30 seconds the Lord told me this is where He wanted us to be. It was funny because my wife and I thought we would shop around for churches, in a manner of speaking. We had plans of visiting a different church each Sunday and then we would make a decision on which church was best for us. I was once again experiencing the fact that God's ways are definitely not our ways. I did not immediately have the courage to tell my wife what the Lord had said.

The story is hysterical in some ways. The next Sunday we visited the same church again. I was enjoying sitting in the back, not having to do anything. I was tired and ready for a little break from the ministry. Toward the end of the service, the pastor looked at us and he invited us up front. I was thinking, what is going on here? He asked us to serve at the altar and pray for people who would come forward. I was thinking, well so much for the break from ministry. After we prayed over several people, the pastor asked us again to come up front and had us face the audience. He then said, "I want everybody to come up here and welcome our two new members Ray and Christie Self." I was in complete shock. My wife looked at me with a look only a wife can give. I knew she was thinking, "What have you done now?" We just smiled as the congregation came up to shake our hands and welcome us as new members. The pastor grew to become a very good friend. When anyone asked me how I came to join this church, I simply said we were drafted. It is very interesting to note I have never seen the pastor do that to anyone else since that time. God had a plan and He literally grabbed hold of us.

Therefore, the key point is the Lord called me to a promised land in Central Florida. Somehow, by the grace of God, I was able to make that move. At first, there was a struggle settling in and making contacts. There was a lot of work to do. I am a full time minister. I had founded the International College of Ministry and I wanted to get it established. I have been in Central Florida now for over five years and I have had more opportunities and more blessings than I could ever imagine. I consider it a privilege to have traveled and ministered from Central Florida in cities all over the United States and Guatemala. My ministry has grown more successful than it has ever been and I have been able to touch more lives for Christ than I could have ever imagined. The International College of Ministry has a large online campus as well as operating in seven cities. Although this is not the plan I had, it is definitely the God-plan for me and it is far greater than anything I could have ever imagined.Because I have lived it, I am excited and thrilled about the subject of finding your promised land. I hope you understand my passion for this topic.

Getting there means you will need to overcome obstacles. In the previous chapters, I have described issues and solutions that are encountered on the road to the promised land. To overcome these issues takes knowledge and courage. I do not know of any mature Christian who wants to be out of the will of God. To get in line with God means we will have to face issues and deal with them in God's way. It will take courage and involve some risks, but the Lord will always be with you.

Review questions –


What has been your most difficult obstacle in getting to your promised land?


Why is obedience to the voice of the Lord important to have victory?


Do you feel called to a specific place? Where is that place? If you are not in that place, then the question is; why not?


In overcoming obstacles, why does it take knowledge and courage?

# Chapter Eleven

## Conquer Your Land

The second stage concerning your promised land is to conquer it. Please understand, this is the place the Lord has given you. Victory will be yours, but you may have to make a stand like King Jehoshaphat and the nation of Judah or you may have to fight to take what is rightfully yours, but in the end, God will give you the victory.

As you go to conquer your promised land, there are some key basic principles you must adhere to.First, it is very important you understand spiritual authority and come under the covering of a church. It is vitalyou become a part of a healthy church. The church the Lord has called you to should be a place where you are fed, nurtured, protected and a place where your gifts and callings are recognized. This should be a place where you have a personal relationship with the pastor. It should be a place where the pastor is not simply a motivational speaker in front of thousands of people and you never actually talk to him. It should be a place where you can go to the pastor and allow him to speak into your life. Your pastor should know you well enough that he understands how to pray for you, how to encourage you and how to help you conquer your promised land. Your pastor should not be a man concerned only about his vision, but it should be a man who will come along beside you and help you with your vision.

My pastor in Orlando, Dr. Joe Warner is an amazing man. He is very apostolic in his nature, but does not see his office as a position above me or anybody else in the church. He sees his call as a call to come along beside people, to work with them, to help them, equip them, heal them, and eventually send them out to whatever God has called them to do. It is very refreshing and very encouraging to be in a church like this. I pray youwill find a similar church, a church where they can care about you and can build and equip you to be all that God has called you to be. Your church needs to be a place that provides warriors to help you fight the battles and conquer yourown promised land. Your church should be a place where you can help nurture and minister to others around you not a place that you feel controlled, but instead a place where you feel safe. The world believes if you submit to authority you will be controlled and not allowed to be all you can be. The exact opposite is true in God's Word. When you submit to the authority God has established in your life, you actually become free. Under godly authority, you gain more freedom, more power, and more grace to do what you are called to do. Under authority, you will accomplish much more than you could do on your own.

Over the years, I have seen many ministers I refer to as lone wolves, believing they have a special call from God, but no church or pastor really understands them. Because of their own insecurities, they will not submit to the local church. Sadly, what I have witnessed in my many years as a Christian is none of these lone wolf ministers ever truly prospers in their calling. The ones that build ministries by themselves, because they have no accountability, eventually fall into some form of deception. I have seen this play out repeatedly. Ministers and Christians who will not submit to authority are easy prey for the devil. It is discouraging to see someone deceived by the enemy of God because when a person is deceived, most often he or she never knows they are deceived simply because 'they are deceived'. What I am asking you to do, regardless of your education or position in life, is to humble yourself and submit to a local church if you have not already done so. What you will experience is that you will have more power, more authority and more freedom than you ever dreamed.

When I came to Orlando and submitted to Pastor Joe Warner, in actuality, the ministry I surrendered in North Mississippi was larger than his ministry. I had every right to believe that, because of my background, perhaps Pastor Warner should have submitted to me. That is not what I wanted to do. I understand and respect the principle of spiritual authority; I submitted my ministry, my family, and myself to my pastor. Soon the level of anointing, prosperity, and success became greater than anything I could have imagined. When you are conquering your promised land, it is imperative that you come under authority. This principle is clear in Scripture. Jesus, in His discourse with the centurion who had the servant who was ill, was amazed at the centurion's faith and understanding of authority. Matthew 8:9-10 says it this way, "For I also am a man under authority, with soldiers under me; and I say to this one, 'Go!' and he goes, and to another, 'Come!' and he comes, and to my slave, 'Do this!' and he does it."Now when Jesus heard this, He marveled and said to those who were following, "Truly I say to you, I have not found such great faith with anyone in Israel."

When Israel came to the land of Canaan, they sent twelve spies out to survey the land. You know the story: ten of the twelve spies came back saying there were giants in the land and it was too much for them to conquer. Only two of the spies came back and said 'yes there are giants in the land, but we know we can conquer this land because the Lord has said so.' The problem was the report of the majority of the spies. Numbers 13:33 says, "There also we saw the Nephilim (the sons of Anak are part of the Nephilim); and we became like grasshoppers in our own sight, and so we were in their sight." Instead of the Israelites seeing themselves as conquerors and being victorious, they saw themselves as small and as weak as grasshoppers. Their personal beliefs and the scheme of illegitimacy blocked them from their promised land.

It is difficult to be a conqueror when you see yourself as defeated. It is difficult to possess something when you turn your back on it. Everything was there waiting for them, but their view of themselves limited God.

*"Yea, they turned back and tempted God, and limited the Holy One of Israel" (Psalms 78:4, KJV).*

You may say God is limitless so how could He be limited? The truth is God is not an enabler. When there is unbelief and disobedience, God will limit His own hand. God wants our trust, our faith, and our obedience. He will not enable us or bless us when we refuse to believe His promises. Hebrews 3:19 says, "So we see that they were not able to enter because of unbelief." Because of Israel's unwillingness to conquer the Promised Land, they were required to go back into the wilderness and wander around for another forty years.

The principle is that when God promises you something, you can have it, even if you have to fight for it. However, God will require your faith in what He has promised you. Victory involves overcoming obstacles. To have your personal victory, you will need to fight your way to your promised land and you will have to fight to conquer that land. No one likes to have a battle, but when you are fighting for God's will and purpose, the battle will be won. God loves faith and your faith will move the hand of God on your behalf. When you trust God for the victory, you will never be fighting in your own strength. Trust in God involves action. When you take steps, God will be with you.

Most of the time, the most fearful part of conquering is just taking the next step. When you are in the battle, God is with you; just take that first step and you will see the beginning of His victory. I promise you the second step will not be nearly as fearful. When you take your steps, you do not know what is going to happen, but when you take a step trusting in God, be assured that even though you do not know the future, the future is victorious. The power that is behind you is far greater that anything in front of you.

I believe there are people right now who are already in their promised land and they are there to maintain it until you get there. In the case of Israel, there were other people living in the land before they got there, which was a good thing. They had farms, buildings, and livestock they took care of. All of this wealth and the necessities were there waiting for the children of God to take possession. There is a land waiting for you and everything you need to prosper and be content is in that land. There may be other people there, temporarily holding onto that wealth until you arrive. If you think about that principle, you can see it operating in America today. We know Christ is coming back and He will set up his kingdom. According to Scripture, Christians will rule and reign with Christ. Unbelievers, as well as believers, are to maintain this land until Jesus comes back to take over. Revelation 5:10 puts it this way, "And hast made us unto our God kings and priests: and we shall reign on the earth."

Christ created the world and everything here is because of Christ; therefore, it is logical that our country with its infrastructure, cities, roads, and economy issomething in place and maintaining until Christ comes back. "Blessed and holy is he that hath part in the first resurrection: on such the second death hath no power, but they shall be priests of God and of Christ, and shall reign with him a thousand years" (Revelation 20:6). Another way of looking at this is the principleof moving into a new home. You decide one day that it is time to purchase a new house, so you search until you find the right one. You close on the deal and then you move in. The house may have been there for years just waiting for you to take possession. The same is true of your promised land; your special place in the will of God is waiting for you to take possession.

Fighting for your promised land is accomplished in many ways. Conquering can involve simply standing still and refusing to be swayed. Conquering can be prayer intercession. Conquering can be spiritual warfare accomplished by proclaiming the truth of God's Word and commanding Satan out of your territory. Victory comes many times by persistence. That means you do not stop, you do not quit, when the storms come, you stubbornly and persistently move ahead despite the obstacles. It means you know how to press through when the distractions and hindrances come your way. The Lord gives another great promise to us in Galatians 6:9, "Let us not lose heart in doing good, for in due time we will reap if we do not grow weary." That is a beautiful promise and it says if we do not stop doing what is right there is a harvest waiting for us. Persistence is always victorious when in obedience to God. When you move into a new home, there is a lot of work to do before you can completely settle down and enjoy it. It is the same with your promised land. There can be a lot of work to do before you can completely enjoy it. If you know your heart, and have listened to the Holy Spirit, and you are in the place God has called you to be, the work will not be difficult.

Conquering your personal promised land takes diligence, prayer, and a willing heart. You must believe the assurance of victory if you do what God has asked you to do. The Lord will never bring you to a promised land to have you fail. When you fight battles, always remember you are not fighting alone. It is you in a covenant with God doing battle together. We all know the story of David and Goliath. What was it that gave David his courage? His courage came from his knowledge of God's covenant. His knowledge gave him faith in his covenant with God. David knew that he was not fighting Goliath alone and said to the Philistine, "You come to me with a sword, a spear, and a javelin, but I come to you in the name of the LORD of hosts" (1 Samuel 17:45). David actually ran toward Goliath with great boldness and courage. "Then it happened when the Philistine rose and came and drew near to meet David, that David ran quickly toward the battle line to meet the Philistine" (1 Samuel 17:48). David understood the principles of covenant when in battle.

One of the key principles of a covenant is there is a promise between the two people to protect each other. When entering a covenant, there is an exchange. Each party in the agreement offers all of his possessions to the other. The promise is like a marriage covenant when the bride and the groom commit all that they have to each other. There is a commitment to give completely to each other and to protect one another. When God established His covenant with us, there was an exchange. Jesus gave His entire life to us in exchange for our lives. This is the essence of covenant. So, when you are in the battle to conquer your promised land, understand you have a covenant with God who is giving you the power and authority of His son, Jesus. You have nothing to fear. Everything with God requires faith. Knowledge creates faith. The more you know, the more you will believe. This is not a book about covenant, but an understanding of covenant is essential for all Christians. There is much written and said about covenant. I encourage the reader to study covenant, especially, the New Testament blood covenant, because understanding this is key to your success or failure in life. David had knowledge of his covenant with God, which gave him courage to face Goliath and win a great victory. When you have knowledge and faith in the covenant you have with the Lord through the sacrifice of Jesus Christ, you will have courage to be victorious against anything the world throws against you.

When I moved to Florida, I had many setbacks. I experienced frustrations and some failures, but I always believed what the Apostle Paul wrote in Galatians 6:9, "And let us not be weary in well doing: for in due season we shall reap, if we faint not." I knew in my heart that if I was persistent and would never give up that I would reap the harvest God had for me. My whole life I have always had a persistent nature. When I was young, I played many sports. My father was a great athlete and sports were a big part of our family. One of the virtues my father instilled in me in athletics was you never give up. So, no matter what the score was I would never quit. Sometimes I was able to make dramatic comebacks because I would never quit. With God, the only way we can make a comeback and get our promised victory is if we never give up. In sports, you may win the game or lose the game because of your persistence, or lack of it. However, with God, you always win when you never give up. When you are in the place God has called you to, please know frustration, failure, and discouragement can happen. Understand every day will not necessarily be a rosy day. Some days can make you feel like giving up hope. A preacher friend of mine said one time he quit the ministry every Monday for 25 years and went on to say, God also laughed at him every Monday for 25 years.

When you are in your purpose and destiny, you have strengths you never imagined. When you are outside of your purpose and destiny, and your strength is simply your own, you tend to burn out. I have often said, if burnout seems to be your problem, then you are probably running on your own fuel. Jesus said in Matthew 11:30, "For my yoke is easy, and my burden is light." This means, what the Lord has called us to do is not hard or difficult. It is actually very logical. If you have ever used tools, you understand the principle that when you are using the right tool for a job the work is much easier. For instance, when you have the correct wrench the bolt loosens very easily. When you use the correct sized Phillips head screwdriver to fit the head of the screw, the screw is easily driven. You are a tool in the toolbox of God and when you are doing the job God designed you for, the job is not hard. What is difficult is when you are trying to do the job not intended for you. When you use a flathead screwdriver on a Phillips head screw, you have a problem. When you try to use a pair of pliers when you need a socket and a ratchet, the job becomes difficult. The point is, you can do the job you have been created to do in the place you have been created to do it, because this is what you are designed to do. You are the perfect tool for the job.

Conquering your promised land means to take possession of what God has given you. It means to overcome obstacles that try to keep you from possessing what the Lord has created for you. God has given you a place. He has given you gifts. He has given you relationships. He has given you authority and covering. It is all there for you if you will possess it. You may have to cast out some demons and have patience to persevere, but this promised land is yours. You may have to do whatever it takes to have what the Lord has for you, but I promise you that the Lord has not offered you something you cannot have. He has not called you to do something you cannot do.

Please understand in the natural mind what the Lord is asking you to do may seem overwhelming. If it is not overwhelming then it is probably not from God. What God has asked you to do is always bigger than youare. The principle is, if you could do it on your own, God would not get the glory, butbecause what you are about to do is bigger and greater than what you could do with your own natural ability, God gets the credit and the kingdom of God is built. I personally could never have imagined what the Lord has asked me to do over the past years. I believe, if God had shown me everything He had for me up front, I would have run away in terror. What God did for me, He will do for you. He will unfold His promise for you one day at a time, one page at a time, or one step at a time. He is not going to show you the end of the journey, but His goal is to show you the next day or the next step, so you will always trust Him. God simply wants you to be willing to move when He says move, go when He says go, and do what He asks you to do. It is an exciting ride and you definitely do not want to miss it.

Review questions –


What are the basic principles or keys to conquering your promised land?


What is the purpose of other people already residing in your promised land?


Why is it essential to understand covenant?

What does God promise if we persevere? What do you think your harvest looks like?

# Chapter Twelve

## Settle in Your Land

So it is all come down to this – you have traveled to your promised land and you have fought battles to secure the land; now it is time to settle down. For some of you, settling down may be difficult, because you were created with the pioneering spirit, but there is a time and a place for everything. "Settling down" means to create your foundation. In this stage, you begin to build a foundation that is solid and with the spirit of excellence. You build a base of operations in which you can travel from to complete the missions God will give you. This settling down phase involves creating security and creating a home base. Everyone needs a place to call home and your promised land should be your home. After you have gotten to it and you have conquered it, you settle down into it.

Settling down can mean setting up systems and organizations. If your promised land involves the ministry, it could be things like setting up your nonprofit organization and getting your 501(c) (3). It means finding the right people or the core people to help you with your vision. Settling down means, you start building your new life. You put everything in order with the spirit of excellence. You build a home on a solid concrete slab.

Years ago when I was working in corporate America, I had a season in my life when I was doing very well financially. I was prospering. I had many material things and from a worldview, I was doing well. One day, unexpectedly, in my heart I heard the Lord say to me, "Ray, you have built your house on sand. It is a house of cards built on sand." I did not want to hear that, but I knew what it meant. It meant the foundation I had created was a self-made foundation. It was not a foundation laid under God's authority instead I had created the foundation and despite all my best efforts, all I had created could and would easily fall. Because I was not solid in Christ at that time and I was not doing the will of God in my life, the Lord allowed my house of cards to fall. When it fell, it fell with a mighty crash and it fell rapidly. Even as it fell, I knew what the Lord had told me. But my God is a good God and out of the ashes, dust and rubble, God began to rebuild a new Ray Self with a new life and ministry, this time built according to His will and in His image.

When you begin to get things in order, or as we like to say, "get your ducks in a row", it actually feels pretty good. Organization relieves stress. The Bible says that God is not the author of confusion and He is not a God of disorder. So build your foundation and do it in an orderly and excellent manner. I have observed over time many Christians with great giftings and callings, but it seems the greatest gift of all is that which is neglected the most of all. I have been around people with prophetic gifting, the gift of healing, and the gift of discernment, which is all wonderful and good, butwhat is sadly lacking is the fruit of the Spirit, which involves character, integrity, and faithfulness.

Through my years in ministry, I have repeatedly witnessed Christians, make commitments, and not complete them. Since we serve an excellent God and we are His children, we should have an excellent spirit. My father was what I call an "old school" type of man. He taught me a principle I never forgot. He said, "Son, a man's word is his bond." What he meant was when a man promises something, he does what he says. Oh, how I would love to see that type of integrity today in the world.

How many times have you heard someone say they will call you back and they never do? Or, they say, I will contact you on Friday and it does not happen. How about, "let's get together for lunch sometime," but sometime is a never time. These seem like small things, but I do not think they are small in the eyes of God. God says in His Word, if we are faithful in little things, He will make us ruler over many things (Matt. 25:21). I really think God watches us in small things such as returning phone calls and living up to commitments or just doing what we say we are going to do. Some of the worst culprits with phone etiquette, unfortunately, are some pastors I know. Getting some ministers to returna phone call is ridiculously hard. Some ministers believe they have arrived and unless you are one of their peers, they may not give you the time of day. Some people only deal with those who can help them. Our God loves all of us and therefore, if we were not able to attend to the least of them, how would He ever allow us to minister to the greatest of them? If were not faithful in little, everyday things and show integrity in small things, how will God ever trust us to show integrity in large things? When you settle into your promised land, it is important for your reputation, and the reputation of God that you are honest and follow through on your word or promises.

A minister or anyone in leadership in the body of Christ is a servant. Leaders are not to be served; but are the ones who are to serve everyone else. This is one of the principles of settling down. We must establish ourselves in the Lord. We need to plant our feet and grow roots in the place God has called us. I love theprinciples in the following scripture. "He will be like a tree firmly planted by streams of water, which yields its fruit in its season and its leaf does not wither; and in whatever he does, he prospers" (Psalms 1:3). The promise is if we stand in the counsel of God and are obedient to Him, we will prosper. A tree planted by a stream has roots that go underground and come out near the edge of the stream where they have a constant supply of life-giving water. Scripturally, water is symbolic of the Holy Spirit. When we are close to the flow of the Holy Spirit, we will never run out of God's life-giving anointing. When we stay in touch with the Holy Spirit, there is a promise that regardless of the season, we will prosper.

No matter what phase of life you are in, understanding the flow and direction of the Spirit of God is vitally important. Without the power of the Holy Spirit, nothing we do apart from God will be effectively. Therefore, whether we are getting to our promised land, conquering our promised land, or settling down in our promised land, we will always need the anointing of the Holy Spirit. A good question to ask yourself is, are you planted where there is an anointing? There are many well meaning traditional churches that have a "form of godliness, but deny the power thereof" (2 Timothy 3:5).

Wherever you settle, it needs to be a place where the anointing is. There is a real simple way to know if the Holy Spirit is moving or if there is an anointing. God is the Creator and He always creates life. The Holy Spirit is the power of God who brings life. If you are in a place that is dead and has no life in it, then you are simply in a place that man has manufactured. Man cannot create life he can only create things. Man can build buildings, roads, cars and computers, but nothing he builds has life. When God is in the house, there is always life. Wherever I am, I use this simple principle to judge if this is where the Holy Spirit is. If I am in a place where there is life, peace, joy, and godliness, then I am in a place the Holy Spirit resides. If I am in a place that looks good, is very nice and well built, but it has a dead feeling about it, I know there is no anointing there. It is very important for you tosettle down where the anointing is. A church with an anointing will always be a church full of life. A church operating with man-made traditions and programs will seem dry and lifeless. To me these types of churches and places are boring. When I am in a place where the Holy Spirit is, I feel peace, I feel joy, I feel love, and it is not boring at all. It may take some trial and error, but work hard to settle down in your promised land, in a place where there is an anointing. In a Wal-Mart or the gas station, there may be no anointing, but there can be an anointing in your home, your church, and there can definitely be an anointing by doing and fulfilling your purpose, whatever that is.

Settling down in your promised land means becoming established. It means finding a good church home and building quality relationships. It means getting organized and it means building a foundation with your core relationships. It involves creating your own special place that you call your own. It is very important you have this place to come back to. Studies have shown one of the most important things a man needs in his life is a peaceful home. Men go out into the world as providers and have many battles to fight there, but there is a time when they just want to come home to a safe and peaceful environment. Some authors have said women are nesters. They love to decorate the home and make it a special place – a place of beauty and comfort where the family can reside in a loving atmosphere. So settling down and having a home base is very important to the man, to the woman and obviously to the family. We all need a place we can launch out from and then come back to. A home should be a place to kick your shoes off and sometimes just relax and do nothing. It is a place to rest, a place to play, and sometimes just simply a place just to be ourselves. Everyone must find that place. If this place you settle down in is your promised land, doing and fulfilling your call from God there will be a truly wonderful and fulfilling place.

When you settle down you will be making contacts, building relationships, and finding people that God has appointed to your life. When you settle down and establish roots, no storm can ever move you or sway you. As I have said before, when you settle down, always be aware of what time it is. The Bible says in the book of Ecclesiastesthat there is a time for everything. "There is an appointed time for everything. And there is a time for every event under heaven" (Ecclesiastes 3:1). In this settled place, you must find the time to rest. You will need a time to play, time to be with your family and you need time just to be with yourself. There is a time to work, there is a time to eat, a time to sleep. It is important you manage your clock well always knowing what time it is because everything in your life has an appropriate time.

An older way of thinking involved making a priority list. In this list, you would put God first, then you would put your family second, you would then place your ministry in third, you might place yourself at forth, your job fifth, and so-on and so-on. This is a very faulty system because with this system, what most people do is spend a few minutes with God in the morning, for instance, and then He is out of the picture and they move onto something else. With the clock method, you have a time for everything in your life. What you do is, put Christ in the middle of everything. The Bible says Christ is not bound by time. He is our centerpiece. He is our heart. He is in the middle of everything. So regardless of what time it is, Christ should be with us. He is not simply first. He is first, last, and everything. That is the way Christians should live.

*"I am the Alpha and the Omega, the first and the last, the beginning and the end" (Revelation 22:13).*

Review questions –

Does your life have a solid foundation? What does having a solid foundation mean to you?

How can you determine if something is man-made or God made?

Why is the fruit of the Spirit vitally important?

Describe the clock method and how it can work in your personal life?

# Chapter Thirteen


## Prosper in Your Land


There has been a lot of controversy in the realm of Christianity concerning prosperity. Over the years,there have been many teachers of the prosperity gospel. Some people have come against them in saying this is nothing but a ploy to justify their own wealth. Some say it is a perversion of the gospel. As for myself, a believer and follower of Christ, I believe the Bible is the Word of God and it should not be taken out of context, and when the Bible is absolutely clear, it should be believed.One of the laws of hermeneutics, the interpretation of Scripture, is that what is clear interprets the vague. Therefore, in this chapter we will look at prosperity and what it means to prosper in your promised land from a clear view of Scripture.

We have been discussing how to get to the place that God has called you to be in your life and what to do when you get there. We have talked about the road to the promised land and the various obstacles and healing that needs to take place to help you get to where you need to be. We have talked about entering into your promised land, conquering your promised land, and then settling down and building a foundation in your promised land. I believe God wants to prosper you and the place He called you to be. I believe the Lord wants you to prosper in all areas of your life. Please understand God's view of prosperity is not always about money. It is also about your body, your spirit, and your soul. As I told you, in my past I had seasons where I had money and seasons where I had very little money. It is very nice to be able to pay your bills and have something left over. It is thoroughly enjoyable to have enough money to be able to travel, take your wife out to dinner, or simply enjoy the wonderful things our country has to offer. I will say life is easier when there is enough money. There is less stress and we do not have to contend with the fear of lack.

*"But seek first His kingdom and His righteousness, and all these things will be added to you" (Matthew 6:33).*

God's principle is very clear and it is all about our focus and our priorities. The world says money should be our focus, along with power and fame which is the world's definition of success. However, God says go after the kingdom of God and then all these things will be added unto you. What God is saying is, if you seek Him and His kingdom and His work and you seek that first and foremost, you will not have to be concerned about practical things. If your attention is on the practical things, such as earning money and having personal achievement, I promise you, as a Christian you will end up frustrated and probably burned out. If your attention and focus is on the Lord and His purposes, loving Him, worshiping Him, and doing what He has called you to do, you will prosper. The principles are very clear. If you seek money, eventually you will end up without it. If you seek God, you will have all you need to live.

*"And my God will supply all your needs according to His riches in glory in Christ Jesus" (Philippians 4:19).*

When I have a financial or any need, I often quote the above scripture. As with many scriptures, however, there is a condition associated with it. The scripture said 'God'would supply all our needs. That is great news, but there is an additional condition. He obviously does it through His own wealth—Christ Jesus. That means that God's supply comes through Christ Jesus. Our life must be in Christ. The Bible says we are hidden in Christ. The word "in" means "to be associated with or connected to". God supplies all our needs when we are associated with Christ, connected to Christ, and Christ is living in us.

In the church of my youth, I learned to believe that Christianity was about barely getting by, being meager and perhaps poor and that was all okay. However,as you study Scripture that does not seem to be what the Bible says. For instance, we know according to the Book of Galatians Jesus has redeemed us from the curse of the law that we might have the blessings of Abraham (Galatians 3:13-14). I think it is important to look at what we have been redeemed from. The law of God is extremely strict. The law says if we disobey any single point of the law, we are under a curse. "For as many as are of the works of the Law are under a curse; for it is written, 'CURSED IS EVERYONE WHO DOES NOT ABIDE BY ALL THINGS WRITTEN IN THE BOOK OF THE LAW, TO PERFORM THEM'" (Galatians 3:10).

The law also says if we are perfectly obedient to the law, we are blessed. Deuteronomy 28:1 says, "Now it shall be, if you diligently obey the LORD your God, being careful to do all His commandments which I command you today, the LORD your God will set you high above all the nations of the Earth. All these blessings will come upon you and overtake you if you obey the LORD your God." This is where Christ comes in. No one, single person in history, other than Jesus Himself, has ever been perfectly obedient to the law. Jesus said some very profound words. He said He did not come to abolish the Law, but He came to fulfill the law. In

Matthew 5:17 He says, "Do not think that I came to abolish the Law or the Prophets; I did not come to abolish but to fulfill."

This is a very practical statement. The law is equivalent to a very large test that no one could pass. In fact, there are 633 laws. The law says if you fail any one of them, you are under a curse. So, in other words, if you completely obeyed632 of God's rules, but you do not obey the 633rd rule, then you failed and are under a curse. One question is, why would God create such a test that no one could pass? Again, the answer is very logical. The law clearly speaks to us that we must have a Savior. There is no possible way for us to please God or obey God in our own ability. Therefore, we must have some help. Our help is our Savior, Jesus Christ who came to fulfill all of God's requirements for us. When we accept Jesus as our Savior and believe with our heart that He died and took all our sins and to the crossand when He rose from the dead, He resurrected us from the dead with Him then His perfect obedience of all of God's requirements is credited to us. Follow the logic: if there are blessings for perfect obedience we could not do on our own, but Jesus did it for us, then these blessings are ours.

The Apostle Paul wrote a lot about righteousness. The word "righteousness," in context with the scripture, means to be in right standing with God. As I said in the above paragraph, to be in right standing with God, you have to be in perfect obedience to the law. Many people mistakenly identify God as this fuzzy, loving teddy bear-type of father in heaven. We may forget God is perfect, holy, righteous, and the perfect moral judge of the universe. If God is absolute perfection and we are not, how can we possibly have an intimate relationship with Him? The Bible says by our nature we are all sinners and God cannot even look upon sin. Again, we come back to Christ who paid the price for all our transgressions. If we believe we are in right standing with God, because of Christ,we have met the requirements of His law, and therefore, we are legally entitled to God's blessing.

*"For in it the righteousness of God is revealed from faith to faith; as it is written, 'BUT THE RIGHTEOUS man SHALL LIVE BY FAITH'" (Romans 1:17).*

The faith that makes me righteous is the faith that believes Jesus Christ took my own unrighteousness to the cross and then imparted to me His righteousness as a gift. It is important to understand your imparted righteousness, because this righteousness has tremendous benefits. The devil does not want you to think you are righteous or in right standing with God. That is why he continues to use guilt, shame, and condemnation to hinder you from all God has for you. The following scripture is a key scripture in my life as it has a lot to say about prosperity.

*"He made Him who knew no sin to be sin on our behalf, so that we might becomethe righteousness of God in Him" (2 Corinthians 5:21).*

This is a two-part scripture. Part One: Jesus became our sin. Part Two: Jesus gave us His righteousness. Think about this He took away everything belonging to us and gave us what belonged to Him. What an amazing gift! It should be a primary reason to praise Jesus everyday of our lives. Now, if I am in right standing with God, then I can boldly go back to Deuteronomy, chapter 28 and look at those verses in a new light. The conditions for the blessings mentioned in this chapter are perfect obedience to God's commandments. If I have Christ's righteousness by faith, then by that same faith I am obedient to God, and have met the requirements for the blessings.

These blessings are absolutely amazing. There are two ways to look at these blessings one beingto look at it is what has been given to you and belongs to you rightly because of Christ and another isto look at it is the cursesof disobedience, which do not belong to you because of Christ. The following scripture sums up the blessings described in Deuteronomy 28.

*"The LORD will make you abound in prosperity" (Deuteronomy 28:11).*

In this chapter, Moses described blessings concerning the work, family, and even concerning victory over enemies. Moses went on to write about the curses for disobedience. Today I read these curses with a different attitude. I like to read these curses so I know what does not belong to me so when the devil tries to put something upon me or in my life that is a part of one of the curses, I know Christ has redeemed me from that and I have a word from God to stand on. As Christians, we have legal rights won for us by Christ, but it is up to us to stand up for what belongs to us.

One very clear curse is this: Deuteronomy 28:44, "He shall lend to you, but you will not lend to him; he shall be the head, and you will be the tail." What the Lord is saying to us is debt is a curse. The Lord is telling us through this curse that when in debt, we will have to borrow just to make it. That is a curse because when you are in debt, the one who loaned you the money is the head and you are the tail. Understanding these curses also allows you to know your redemption. We are children of the King of kings and Lord of lords. In essence, God does not want harm to come upon us and He does not want us to be in lack for anything. Most of you who are reading this probably have children of your own. Do you desire for your own kids to lack or prosper? If God is love and He loves us more than we could ever imagine, it is simply illogical that God's will is for us to be in lack and debt. I want to make it clear abundance is not simply having money it is in the peace and contentment of being in your promised land and being in the will of God for your life.

I have told you before I have had plenty of money in previous times in my life, but I was not happy because I was looking for money to bring me what it could not do. What I have found is that my joy comes from the Lord and by working to fulfill His purpose for me. When I get to my promised land and do what I am to do, the Lord provides for every need I have. I believe strongly that it is the Lord's will for us to prosper in every area of our life. He wants us to prosper in relationships, prosper in our family, prosper in ministry, prosper in our job, and yes, even to prosper financially.

Knowing your source is the key to prosperity. God is the source of all wealth. We are simply managers of this wealth. When you have that attitude of managing faithfully the resources God has given you, He will give you more resources than you could ever imagine. However, if you believe you are the one in charge and your job is to make good money and be responsible for the financial well- being of yourself and your family, then you will simply dry up. Without an acknowledgement and dependency of God, you will be in trouble. God is not an enabler and He will not bless us when we work outside of His will.

As you enter into this phase of your life, when you have found your purpose and discovered what you are to do and you have conquered and settled down, I encourage you to enjoy every single day. Settling down means, you are in a solid protected place in your life. Settling down means,you have worked through the issues and the hindrances and you have come to a place in your life that you know what you are to do and you are doing it in the right place and time. Enjoy the peace and contentment and enjoy, especially, the impact you will have on your family your friends in your community when you are settled within your promised land. To settle down means you have come to a place where you could build healthy patterns in your life. In this settled place, you can have healthy routines that are good for you and those around you. Remember when you take care of yourself, not only do you benefit, but all of those around you benefit as well.

Getting into God's will for your life is a battle, but it is a battle you win because it is a battle God wants you to win. Please do not be discouraged if after reading this you feel, "Wow, I am so far away from what God has called me to do." I want you to know you are never too far away or too far gonefor God to reach you. No matter what road you are on, God can give you a pathway to get onto His road for you.

A few years ago, I had a funny thing happen to me on a trip. It may have been one of those situations where 'you just had to be there' to see the humor of it all, but allow me to share. I was traveling through southeast Alabama trying to get to Birmingham when I somehow missed a turn and went a few miles the wrong way. I saw a sign for cut off through the town of Auburn. I thought this road would probably eventually get me back to the road I needed to be on so I took the turn and drove a few miles down the highway. The road led me directly into the center of Auburn University when classes were getting out. I sat in my car in the middle of Auburn University unable to move, surrounded by thousands of students making their way to their next class. I thought it was kind-of funny and I definitely felt out of place as I watched the young people looking at me wondering what I was doing there. To make things more interesting, my license plate has an Ole Miss frame around it because my daughter graduated from there. I was really a stranger in a strange land for sure. However, I persisted, managed to get through, and continued on the highway. Even though it was not, the best, shortcut in the world, it did get me back to the road I needed. I hope you understand, no matter where you are there is a way to get back on the right path. A wrong turn can eventually get you to the right place even though you may be a stranger in a strange land for a while.

Review questions –


What does God promise us if we seek Him and His kingdom first in our lives?


Why is it important to understand that Christ has redeemed us from the curse of the law? (Galatians 3:13)


How does Deuteronomy, chapter 28 apply to your personal life?

Why is 'understanding your source' a key to prosperity?

Final assignment for ICM students - List three key points from each chapter of this book and write a summary of this book by explaining each of your key points.

# About the Author

**Dr. Ray Self,** founder of Spirit Wind Ministries Inc. and the International College of Ministry, holds a Doctorate in Christian Psychology and a Doctorate in Theology. The International College of Ministry has campuses in seven cities and a full online college. He also planted the International College of Ministry in the Philippines, Peru, and India. He is the former Pastor and founder of Spirit Wind Ministries Church in Olive Branch, MS. He has appeared on TBN and previously had a weekly radio show in Memphis, TN. Dr. Self has authored several workbooks including Doctrine of The Holy Spirit, Essential Christian Doctrines, and Maturing of the Saints. He is a former international board member for Jacksonville Theological Seminary. He currently resides in Orlando Florida, the location of International College of Ministry's International Headquarters. He is married to Dr. Christie Self and has three sons and a daughter.

## International College of Ministry is a truly unique seminary

A seminary should seek not only to impart knowledge of the word of God, but should also allow the Holy Spirit to lead and impart the power necessary for true revelation of Christ. Just as Christ was "full of grace and truth" (John 1:14), a seminary should be a marriage between the Spirit and the truth. This is what we at the International College of Ministry seek to do. We purpose by the will of God to teach sound biblical doctrine, allowing the Holy Spirit to lead us in all that we do. We are an in-depth ministry training school for those seeking degrees, ordinations, ministry licenses, and a place inspiring personal growth for those wanting a deeper walk with the Lord. It is very easy to get started with us, and our programs are very affordable. A degree program can be completely accomplished online. ICM is a quality seminary recognized by the Florida Department of Education Commission for Independent Education as a religious school.

Visit our website at www.icmcollege.org

The International College of Ministry is a division of Spirit Wind Ministries, Inc. a 501 (c) (3) non-profit corporation. We are a publicly supported registered charity. Tax-deductible donations may be sent to ICM, 311 Saint Dunstan Way, Winter Park, FL 32792. Or at our website www.icmcollege.org click on the *Donate* button on the bottom of the page. May God richly bless you.

Made in the USA
Columbia, SC
05 February 2018